Texas

MAPPING THE LONE STAR STATE THROUGH HISTORY

Detail of map on page 4.

Texas

MAPPING THE LONE STAR STATE THROUGH HISTORY

Rare and Unusual Maps from the Library of Congress

Vincent Virga

and Don Blevins

Guilford, Connecticut

Text design: Sheryl P. Kober
Layout: Casey Shain
Project manager: John Burbidge

Library of Congress Cataloging-in-Publication Data

Virga, Vincent.
 Texas : mapping the lone star state through history : rare and unusual maps from the Library of Congress / Vincent Virga and Don Blevins.
    p. cm.
 Includes bibliographical references.
 ISBN 978-0-7627-4532-6
 1. Texas—Historical geography—Maps. 2. Texas—History—Maps. 3. Early maps—Texas—Facsimiles. 4. Texas—Maps, Manuscript—Facsimiles. I. Blevins, Don, 1933– II. Title.

 GI371.SIV6 2010
 911'.764—dc22

2009582742

Printed in China

10 9 8 7 6 5 4 3 2 1

Contents

Foreword

THE ENDEARING PAROCHIALISM OF A STATE'S IDENTITY (as opposed to a nation's) that forms the self-image of its citizenry—"I am a TEXAN!"—is understandable to me as a native New Yorker, but it might be puzzling to many of my fellow Americans. However, Don Blevins has managed to gracefully parse the unique national myths that have created the Texas mystique. Fighting its own war for independence from Mexico and being a stand-alone nation before becoming a state, inventing the great cattle drives and the legendary American cowboy, giving us a regional archetype of the "Big Rich" oilmen (and conservative political powerhouses), shifting wealth in America away from the East Coast, and sending three native sons to the White House makes Texas culture a thrilling homegrown narrative for every American, not only prideful Texans. This is the American Dream writ large: Texas style!

Living on planet Earth has always raised certain questions. Of course, the most obvious one is, where am I? Well, as Virginia Woolf sagely noted in her diary, writing things down makes them more real, and this may have been a motivating factor for the Old Stone Age artists who invented the language of signs on the walls of their caves in southern France and northern Spain between thirty-seven thousand and eleven thousand years

ago. Picasso reportedly said of them, "They've invented everything," which includes the very concept of an image.

A map is an image. It makes the world more real for us and uses signs to create an essential sense of place in our imagination. (There are petroglyphic maps inscribed in the late Iron Age on boulders high in the Valcamonica region of northern Italy.) Cartographic imaginings not only locate us on this earth but also help us invent our personal and social identities, since maps embody our social order. Like the movies, maps helped create our national identity—though cinema had a vastly wider audience—and this encyclopedic series of books aims to make manifest the changing social order that invented the United States, which is why it embraces all fifty states.

Each is a precious link in the chain of events that is the history of our "great experiment," the first and enduring federal government ingeniously deriving its just powers—as John Adams proposed—from the consent of the governed. Each state has a physical presence that holds a unique place in any representation of our republic in maps. To see each one rise from the body of the continent conjures up Tom Paine's excitement over the resourcefulness, the fecundity, the creative energy of our Enlightenment philosopher-founders: "We are brought at once to the point of seeing government begin, as if we had lived in the beginning of time." Just as the creators systematized not only laws but also rights in our Constitution, so our maps show how their collective memory inspired the body politic to organize, codify, and classify all of nature to do their bidding with passionate preferences state by state. For they knew, as did Alexander Pope,

> All are but parts of one
> stupendous Whole
> Whose body Nature is, and
> God the soul.

And aided by the way maps under interrogation often evoke both time and space, we editors and historians have linked the reflective historical overviews of our nation's genesis to the seduction of place embedded in the art and science of cartography.

J. B. Harley posits, "The history of the map is inextricably linked to the rise of the nation-state in the modern world." The American bald eagle has been the U.S. emblem since 1782, after the Continental Congress appointed a committee in 1776 to devise an official seal for our country. (The eagle was the ancient personification of Zeus and, by extension, supreme authority. Hatched in the midst of war, however, our symbolic eagle clutches arrows in one claw but an olive branch in the other.) The story of our own national geographical writing begins in the same period but has its roots centuries earlier, appropriately, in a flock of birds.

On October 9, 1492, after sailing westward for four weeks in an incomprehensibly vast and unknown sea during North America's migration month, an anxious Christopher Columbus spotted an unidentified flock of migrating birds flying south and signifying land—"Tierra! Tierra!" Changing course to align his ships with this overhead harbinger of salvation, he avoided being drawn into the northern-flowing Gulf Stream, which was waiting to be charted by Ben Franklin around the time our eagle became America as art. And so, on October 11, Columbus encountered the southern end of San Salvador. Instead of landing somewhere in the future New England, he came up the lee of the island's west coast to an easy and safe anchorage.

Lacking maps of the beachfront property before his eyes, he assumed himself in Asia because in his imagination there were only three parts to the known world: Europe, Asia, and Africa. To the day he died, Columbus doubted he had come upon a fourth part even though Europeans had already begun appropriating through the agency of maps what to them was a New World, a new continent. Perhaps the greatest visual statement of the general confusion that rocked the Old World as word spread of Columbus's interrupted journey to Asia is the Ruysch map of 1507. Here we see our nascent home inserted into the template created in the second century by Ptolemy, a mathematician, astrologer, and geographer of the Greco-Roman known world, the *oikoumene.*

This map changed my life. It opened my eyes to the power of a true cultural landscape. It taught me that I must always *look* at what I *see* on a map, focusing my attention on why the map was made, not who made it, when or where it was made but *why.* The Ruysch map was made to circulate the current news. It is a quiet meditative moment in a very busy, noisy time. It is life on the cusp of a new order. And the new order is what historian

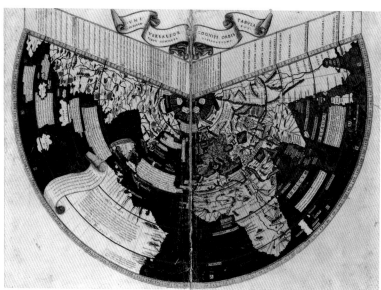

Ruysch map, 1507

Henry Steele Commager christened the "uto-pian romance" that is America. No longer were maps merely mirrors of nature for me. No longer were the old ones "incorrect" and ignorant of the "truth." No longer did they exist simply to orient me in the practical world. The Ruysch map is reality circa 1507! It is a time machine; it makes the invisible past visible. Blessedly free of impossible abstractions and idealized virtues, it is undeniably my sort of primary historical document.

The same year, 1507, the Waldseemüller map appeared. It is yet another reality and one very close to the one we hold dear. There we Americans are named for the first time. And there we sit, an independent continent with oceans on both sides of us, six years *before* Balboa supposedly discovered "the other sea." There are few maps as mysterious for cartographic scholars as Wald-seemüller's masterpiece. Where did all that news come from? For our purposes it is sufficient to say to the world's visual imagination, "Welcome to us Americans in all our cartographic splendor!"

Throughout my aca-demic life maps were never offered to me as primary historical documents. When I became a picture editor, I learned to my amazement that most book editors are logocentric, or "word people." Along with most historians and academ-ics, they make their liveli-hoods working with words and ideas. For a traditional historian maps are merely archival devices dealing with scientific accuracy. They cannot "see" a map as a first-person, visual narrative crammed with very particular insights into the process of social history. However, the true nature of maps as a key player in the history of the human imagination is a cornerstone of our series.

The very title of this volume, *Texas: Mapping the Lone Star State through History,* makes it clear that this series has a specific agenda, as does each map. It aims to thrust us all into a new intimacy with the American experience by detailing the creative process of our nation in motion through time and space via word *and* image. It grows from the relatively recent shift in consciousness about the physical, mental, and spiritual relevance of maps in our understanding of our lives on Earth. Just as each state is an integral part of the larger United States, "Where are we?" is a piece of the larger puzzle called "Who are we?"

The Library of Congress was founded in 1800 with 740 volumes and three maps. It has

Waldseemüller map, 1507

grown into the world's largest library and is known as "America's Memory." For me its vast visual holdings, made by those who helped build this nation, make the library the eyes of our nation as well. There are nearly five million maps in the Geography and Map Division. We have linked our series with that great collection in the hopes that its astonishing breadth will inspire us in our efforts to strike Lincoln's "mystic chords of memorys" and create living history.

On January 25, 1786, Thomas Jefferson wrote, "Our confederacy must be viewed as the nest from which all America, North and South is to be peopled." This is a man who could not live without books, a man who drew maps. This is a politician who in spite of his abhorrence of slavery and his respect for Native Americans took pragmatic rather than principled positions when confronted by both "issues." Nonetheless,

his bold vision of an expanded American universe informs our current enterprise. There is no denying that the story of the United States has a dark side, but what makes the American narrative unique is the ability we have displayed time and again to remedy our mistakes, to adjust to changing circumstances, to debate and then move on in new directions that seem better for all.

For Jefferson (whose library was the basis for the current Library of Congress after the British burned the first one during the War of 1812) and for his contemporaries, the doctrine of progress was a keystone of the Enlightenment. The maps in our books are reports on America, and all their political programs are manifestations of progress. Our starting fresh, free of old-world hierarchies, class attitudes, and the errors of tradition, is wedded to our geographical isolation, with its immunity from the endless internal European wars that were devastating humanity. They justify Jefferson's confessing, "I like the dreams of the future better than the history of the past." But as the historian Michael Kammen explains, "For much of our history we have been present-minded; yet a usable past has been needed to give shape and substance to national identity." Historical maps keep the past warm with life and immediately around us. They encourage critical enquiry, curiosity, and qualms.

For me this series of books celebrating each of our states is not about the delineation of property rights. It is a depiction of the pursuit of happiness, which is listed as one of our natural rights in the 1776 Declaration of Independence. (Thirteen years later when the French revolutionaries drafted a Declaration of the Rights of Man, they included "property rights," and Jefferson unsuccessfully urged them to substitute "pursuit of happiness" for "property.") Jefferson also believed that "the earth belongs always to the living generation." I believe these books depict what each succeeding generation in its pursuit of happiness accomplished on this portion of the earth known as the United States. If America is a matter of an idea, then maps are an image of that idea.

I also fervently believe these books will show the states linked in the same way Lincoln saw the statement that all men are created equal as "the electric cord in that Declaration that links the hearts of patriotic and liberty-loving men together, that will link those patriotic hearts as long as the love of freedom exists in the mind of men throughout the world."

Vincent Virga
Washington, D.C.
Inauguration Day, 2009

Introduction

In January 1821, when the Spanish, and later the Mexicans, agreed to Moses Austin's petition to establish a colony of three hundred Catholic settlers in a region of what is now southeast Texas along the Colorado River, they had no way of knowing the Pandora's box they were opening. That fateful decision changed the history of Mexico and the United States. It also gave rise to an entity that would survive conflict, become a republic, and in a short time see its star sewn on the American flag.

Benevolence on the part of the Spanish and the Mexicans had nothing to do with allowing Anglos into their northern territory. Authorities in Mexico were impressed with the way Anglos handled their American Indian "problems" in the East and with how efficient they were at establishing settlements. Furthermore, they held hope that Anglo colonists in Texas would serve as a buffer against further migration from the United States.

On August 24, 1821, Spain signed the Treaty of Córdoba, which granted Mexico independence from the European power. With some trepidation, and for the same reasons as Spain, Mexico City continued the colonization agreement with Moses Austin's son Stephen. Austin assumed the mantle of *empresario* and brought in settlers, who became known as the Old Three Hundred.

Those Anglos had no problems becoming Mexican citizens, as required by law, which meant that they had to convert to Catholicism (though many took the oath with their fingers crossed)—their interest was in the land. Relations were fairly stable between Mexico City and its Texas province, but in time recommendations came from south of the Rio Grande to clamp down on the American settlers' freedoms. It was feared by some Mexican officials that the Anglos would foment uprisings that would spread south into Mexico's heartland.

A restrictive law passed on April 6, 1830, prohibited further immigration from the United States, outlawed bringing slaves into the territory, and ended *empresario* contracts. Meant to restrict the settlers' activities and stunt any growth in number, this act set the colonists on edge, but like Austin, they were willing to bide their time and hope the law would be overturned. Six years later, however, the new restrictions were the catalyst for the Texas Revolution.

The Anglo colonists, who had become known as Texians, became more belligerent about independence, and Mexico City was just as firmly set against losing its northern province. Mexican military authorities felt the only way to control the Texians and their allies, the Tejanos (people living in Texas of Mexican descent), was through military force or occupation.

Although Texian leaders voted to pursue peace but to prepare for war if necessary, the first shots of the revolution took place on October 2, 1835, at Gonzales, some seventy miles east of San Antonio, when Mexican forces attempted to retrieve a cannon given the citizens as protection against hostile Native Americans. The townspeople refused to return the weapon and displayed a homemade flag emblazoned, "COME AND TAKE IT." Their military rebuff was sufficient, and the Mexicans returned to San Antonio. On October 9 General Martín Perfecto de Cos, brother-in-law of General Santa Anna, occupied San Antonio. A Texian-Tejano force attacked the general on December 9 and forced the troops back across the Rio Grande.

Santa Anna, his hatred for Anglos knowing no bounds and now reinforced by the insult to his family honor, swore vengeance on the Texians and Tejanos and on anyone who defied the laws of Mexico City. Following the massacre at Goliad and the fall of the Alamo, considered wins for Mexico, Santa Anna turned in pursuit of Sam Houston and the so-called Texian army. The two met at San Jacinto, near today's Houston. In an eighteen-minute battle on April 21, 1836, Texas gained tenuous independence from Mexico and became the Republic of Texas, entering yet another fascinating period in the journey to statehood.

When, on December 24, 1845, Texas was admitted to the American Union as the twenty-eighth state, Mexico, which had never officially accepted Texas's independence, considered the annexation an act of war. American troops gathered at the Rio Grande, and Mexico, outfought at nearly every turn, was forced to surrender. The Treaty of Guadalupe Hidalgo, signed in February 1848, established the Rio Grande River as an international boundary. The United States also acquired California, New Mexico, Arizona, Utah, Nevada, Wyoming, and part of Colorado from Mexico for $15 million. In addition, Mexico relinquished all claims to Texas.

When the South seceded from the Union during the Civil War, Texas went with it—and Texas men went to fight. Texans returned to find their home, like other Confederate states, devastated. But Texas had something other states did not—cattle. Bovines had run wild during the four years of the war and increased significantly in number. Easterners were anxious to serve meat once again, and Texans were more than willing to satisfy that craving. Large trail drives moved north to railheads in Kansas and Missouri, and the legendary image of the cowboy emerged. Cattle drives ended about twenty years after they started—by the late 1800s trains had reached Texas, nullifying the long, dusty drives.

It was a very short time between the demise of the cattle drives and the next event that would continue the Texas mystique. Oil had been discovered in the 1800s in Texas, but nothing compared to the Spindletop gusher of 1901. While Spindletop spewed out millions of dollars worth of black gold, other wells were discovered in East and West Texas, which added to the aura of Texas "oilinaires." Even when oil began its slow decline in price, and the country started importing more and more from overseas, the picture of the Texas oilman in his fancy car and large mansion still prevails; the movie *Giant,* based on Edna Ferber's classic novel, took hold of the imagination and stayed there.

World Wars I and II brought "newness" to the Lone Star State, a newness of population, military structures, and defense spending. Many military personnel who were stationed in Texas during WWII either remained after the war or returned. Some married locally and put down roots.

Today there is still oil, just not as much. The King Ranch and other cattle ranches are scattered throughout West Texas. Military bases are a vital part of the heart and soul of the state. To all this has been added high-tech industries, space-exploration facilities, and myriad other industries. And of course, football has become a part of the Texas identity with the Dallas Cowboys, "America's Team," and the stories of "Friday Night Lights."

These essays and maps provide only a thumbnail sketch of the rise of the Lone Star State. Each in its own way helps explain the aura surrounding the 267,339 square miles within its border.

Tabula Mexicae et Floridae: terrarum Anglicarum, et anteriorum Americae insularum, item cursuum et circuituum fluminis Mississipi dicti, Peter Schenk (1710).

Cartographer Peter Schenck created this map depicting the Gulf of Mexico and portions of North and Central America around 1710. The long finger of land jutting between the Florida peninsula and Mexico's Yucatán Peninsula is Cuba. The island would serve as the port of departure for exploration of Central and South America and would eventually be the jumping-off spot for Spanish expeditions northward into Spanish Texas and beyond. That huge land mass would become, in less than three centuries, the United States.

The Spanish and Mexican Eras

WHEN CHRISTOPHER COLUMBUS SAILED INTO THE Caribbean Sea and established a colony on Hispaniola, later Santo Domingo, in 1493, it was probably the greatest geographical discovery of all time, an event that would change history as few events ever have. At the outset Spain was content claiming, exploiting, and populating the islands to the east of the large land mass now known as North and South America, but the Spanish began their exploration of the North American mainland in 1518. Hernán Cortés persuaded Diego Velázquez, the Spanish governor of Cuba, to turn his interests westward, for more lands to conquer and more wealth to accumulate. Cortés was convincing, and in March 1519, with a force of some six hundred men, he landed in Mexico. They were allowed to explore and claim all South American lands except Brazil, which a previous treaty had granted to Portugal. Although the native population vastly outnumbered the invading Spanish, primitive bows and arrows were futile against metal armament and gunpowder. When brought to bear and combined with the white man's diseases, to which the natives had no immunity, they did not stand a chance of repelling the new arrivals. The Spanish had horses, which made them mobile, while the natives were restricted in their mobility. The horses stunned the Indians, who had never seen such animals.

The Spaniards conquered all of South America, with Diego de Almagro and Francisco Pizarro overcoming the Incas and taking control of Peru. The Aztec empire fell to Cortés, who then turned his attention northward in one of the many quests for the legendary El Dorado or "City of Gold." The conquerors did it all to serve God and get rich, not necessarily in that order. Some Spaniards, both invaders and those back in Spain, did become wealthy; most did not.

There had been explorations of the North American land mass that predated those carried out by Cortés. In 1513 Juan Ponce de León, searching for the elusive fountain of youth, was on the Florida peninsula; and around the same time Vasco Núñez de Balboa set foot on the Isthmus of Panama. Travels and settlements by the Spanish continued through the next three centuries.

The Spanish made forays into North American territories, including Texas, over the next two hundred years. Alonzo Àlvarez de Piñeda is credited with being the first Spaniard to see Texas, but he did so from the deck of his ship. He mapped the coastline and upon returning to Mexico recommended that a colony be established in the region. Pánfilo de Narváez and his expedition landed on Texas soil, but by accident. Around 1519 or 1520 Narváez led a scouting expedition to Florida. He expected Spanish ships to meet them upon completion of their exploration and return them to Cuba, but Narváez was late getting to the rendezvous point, and the ships left without them.

To return to his home port, the commander and his men built wooden rafts and sailed along the gulf coast until November 5, 1528, when strong winds blew them onto an island that they called *Isla de Malhado*, "the island of misfortune." (The site is believed to be today's Galveston Island, although some historians think the men were stranded on San Luis Island, a dot of land west of Galveston. San Luis no longer exists, having been wiped out by early storms.)

Narváez died when the boat he was in sank during a storm; command fell to Àlvar Núñez Cabeza de Vaca. The men who survived were fortunate to be found by friendly Karankawa Indians. For some seven years the group wandered the wastelands of south Texas, sometimes aided by friendly natives and other times, naked and beaten, used as slaves. Finally, making their escape from a group of unfriendly natives, de Vaca led his men back toward their home base. The exact route they traveled is uncertain, but for two years after escaping their captors, they roamed unfamiliar territory. Finally, after traveling by foot for more than 2,000 miles, the men were found by a Spanish patrol at Culiacán in early 1536. (Culiacán is near the Gulf of California, about 125 miles north of Mazatlán.) Of the four hundred men who started out with Narváez, only four, including de Vaca, were alive when they arrived back in Mexico.

Over the years Spaniards made many other expeditions into Texas from south of the Rio Grande. Father Marcus de Niza traveled north with Estavanica, a black slave who was one of the four survivors of the Narváez excursion and who served as guide for the priest. In 1540 Francisco Vásquez de Coronado marched north. Hernando de Soto led his men into Texas at about the same time. Juan de Oñate fronted an expedition in 1598. These expeditions had as their aim the search for the fabled "cities of gold." When gold failed to materialize, the expeditions ceased to interest Spain, which considered the establishing settlements in the vast wasteland (from their point of view) nonproductive. But the ventures did cement Spain's claim on the Texas territory and lands that ran westward to the Pacific Ocean.

Though the Spanish found little to draw their interest in occupation of the area and much to repel them—namely, hostile tribes—they held onto the area primarily because it served as a buffer between its territory and the encroachment of French and Americans from the east. Settlement of Texas by Spaniards living south of the Rio Bravo (Rio Grande) was sparse, with San Antonio being the only settlement of any size. However, on January 17, 1821, authorities in Mexico City granted permission for Moses Austin, an Anglo claiming Mexican citizenship, to settle three hundred American Catholic families in what is today southeastern Texas.

This sudden acceptance of foreign settlement on Spanish territory was not an act of benevolence on the part of Spain. Authorities were impressed at how Anglos had settled and created communities in their part of the continent. They were also interested in how the settlers coped with, and were coping with, their Indian "problems."

Furthermore, Spain hoped that settlement by a limited number of Anglos in Spanish Texas could serve as another bulwark against incursions from the French and the Anglos.

When Spain began to suffer militarily and financially because of the rampages of Napoleon Bonaparte in Europe, the government in Madrid had to levy heavy taxes on the citizens of *La Nuevo España* (New Spain). As expected, this did not sit well with the people of Mexico. On September 16, 1810, Father Miguel Hidalgo y Costilla issued his *El Grito* ("The Cry"), which was a call for rebellion against the Spanish overlords. The Mexican struggle for autonomy ended victoriously for the rebels when, on August 24, 1821, Spanish representatives signed the Treaty of Cordova.

Mexican authorities decided to recognize the agreement with the Anglos for settlement in what was now Mexican Texas and for the same reasons Spain had agreed to it. As for the Anglos, who had been putting down roots in Texas as early as 1815, the problems taking place south of the Rio Grande interested them little, if at all. Their concern was garnering a living and acquiring property. The motto GTT (Gone to Texas) not only meant escaping problems at home but starting a new life elsewhere and possibly becoming financially affluent at the same time. The Anglos were pretty much left to their own devices, with little interference from authorities in Mexico and with a near nonexistent tax load. This would soon change, however.

Antonio López de Santa Anna, the self-proclaimed "Napoleon of the West," was once again *el presidente* of Mexico. His abrogation of the Mexican Constitution of 1824 set the stage for the Anglo rebellion in Mexican Texas.

A map of Louisiana and of the river Mississipi [i.e. Mississippi], by Iohn Senex (1721).
Created in the 1720s and published in London, and clearly depicting the coastline of Texas along the Gulf of Mexico, this map demonstrates the knowledge that all of Europe was gathering about the Louisiana Territory and the vast interior of the North American continent as the superpowers of the day battled for control over its resources.

A new & accurate map of Louisiana, with part of Florida and Canada, and the adjacent countries. Drawn from surveys, assisted by the most approved English & French maps & charts, the whole being regulated by astronl. observations, by Eman. Bowen (1752).

Emanuel Bowen's map of 1752 shows the area from the Gulf of Mexico to northern Canada. Lands east of the Mississippi River belonged to France; to the west were Spain's. France claimed lands extending westward from Placentia, Newfoundland, through Canada, the Great Lakes, and the Mississippi Valley to the Gulf of Mexico. France lost control of the region through the French and Indian wars, with the British backing the Indians. The Great War for Empire ran from 1689 to 1763. The 1763 Treaty of Paris ceded to Britain all lands east of the Mississippi except Louisiana, which France gave to Spain; Cuba once again became a Spanish possession.

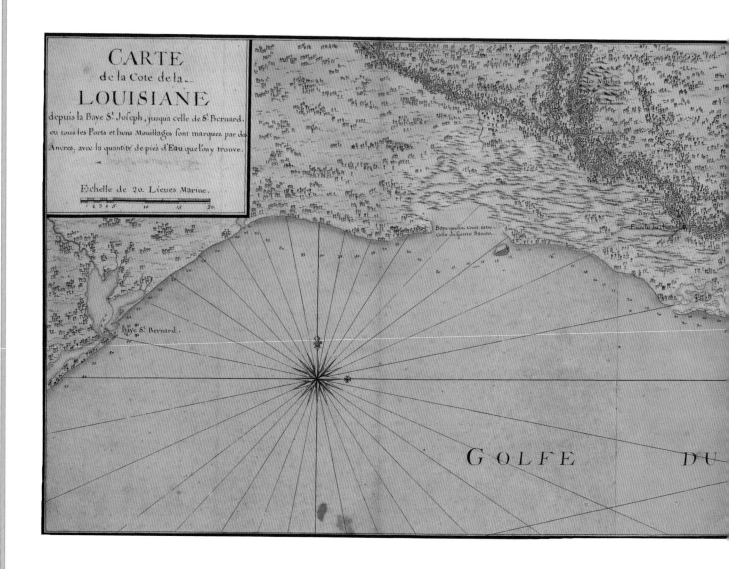

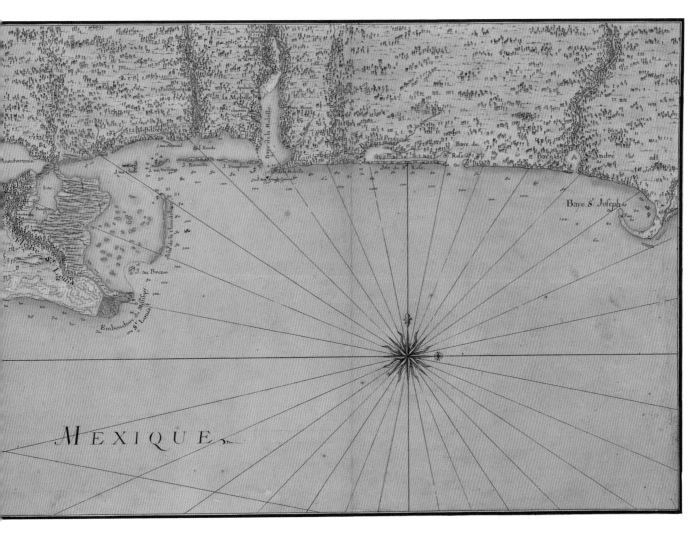

Carte de la côte de la Louisiane depuis la Baye St. Joseph, jusqu'à celle de St. Bernard où tous les ports et bons mouillages sont marquez par des ancres; avec la quantité de piés d'eau que l'on y trouve, creator unknown (1732?).

This map, circa 1732, depicts the Gulf of Mexico. After Narváez and his crew missed the ships that were supposed to return them to Cuba, they built rickety rafts and from the panhandle of Florida sailed westward, staying close to the coastline. Little did they realize it would be a journey of some 600 miles back to their destination. They were blown onto an island by a storm on November 5, 1528. The island on which they landed was either Galveston (at 94° latitude) or the nearby dot of land called San Luis, which no longer exists.

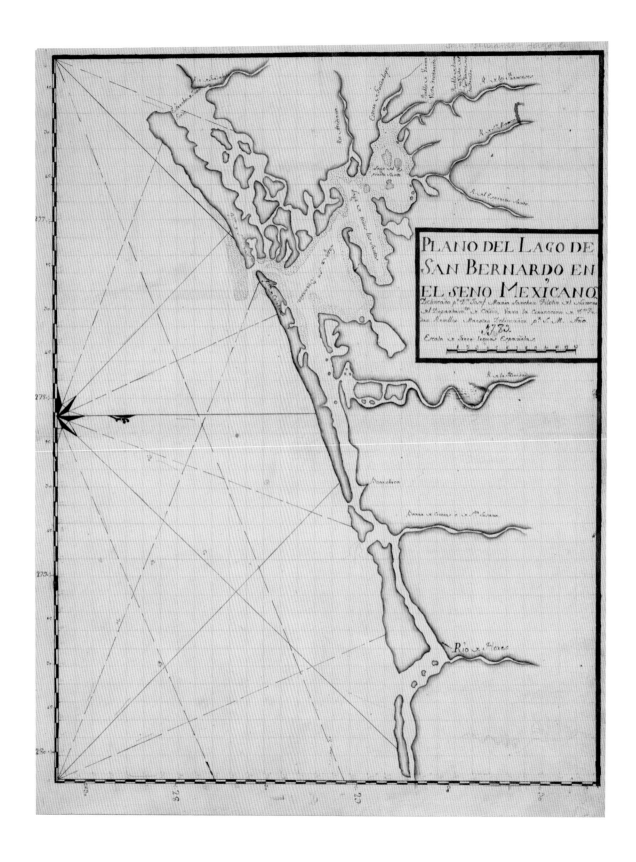

Plano del Lago de San Bernardo en el Seno Mexicano, delineado pr.
Dn. Josef María Sánchez, pilotin del numero del Departamto. de Cádiz,
vaxo la corrección de Dn. Pedro Revelles, maestro delineador pr. S.M.(1783).
In this Josef María Sánchez map, published in 1783, north is on the right. The long strip of land in the center is Matagorda Island; north is the entrance to San Antonio Bay. The Guadalupe River flows into the bay. Early Spanish exploration of the river area began in 1755. A small settlement arose along the river in 1808, but Indians and floods doomed the project. Martín de Léon established the village of Victoria in 1824, and the following year James Kerr founded Gonzales, 60 miles north of San Antonio Bay. The first shot of the Texas Revolution was fired in Gonzales on October 2, 1835.

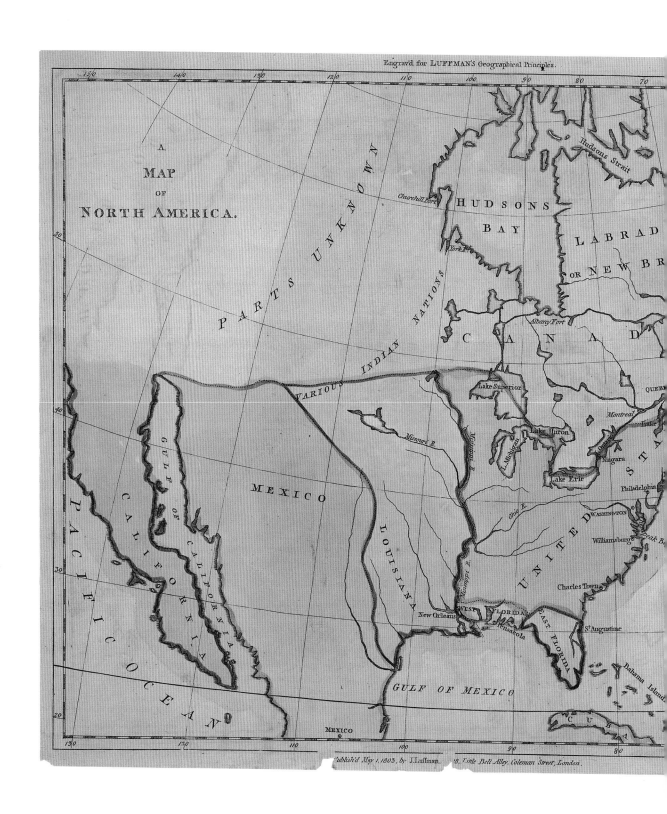

A
MAP
OF
NORTH AMERICA.

PARTS UNKNOWN

HUDSONS
BAY

LABRAD
OR NEW BR

Churchill Fort

York Ft.

Albany Fort

C A N A D

QUEBE

Lake Superior

Montreal

VARIOUS INDIAN NATIONS

Missouri R.

L. Michigan

Lake Huron

Lake Erie

Niagara

Philadelphia

GULF OF CALIFORNIA

M E X I C O

Ohio R.

WASHINGTON

U N I T E D   STA

Williamsburg

CALIFORNIA

LOUISIANA

Mississippi R.

Charles Town

PACIFIC OCEAN

New Orleans

WEST FLORIDA

EAST FLORIDA

St Augustine

Pensacola

Bahama Island

GULF OF MEXICO

MEXICO

C U B A

Publish'd May 1, 1803, by J.Luffman, 98, Little Bell Alley, Coleman Street, London.

A map of North America, John Luffman (1803).

When this John Luffman map was published in 1803, Napoleon's plans for regaining control of the Caribbean island of Hispaniola were thwarted; consequently, the European warlord had no need for Louisiana. President Thomas Jefferson sent representatives to Paris to negotiate for open travel on the Mississippi River. When Napoleon offered the entire Louisiana territory, the Americans jumped at the opportunity. On December 20, 1803, the United States took official control of Louisiana. For some $15 million, the United States acquired 800,000 square miles of territory, doubling its size and setting the fledgling United States on a crash course with Spain for control of the southern territory that would become Texas.

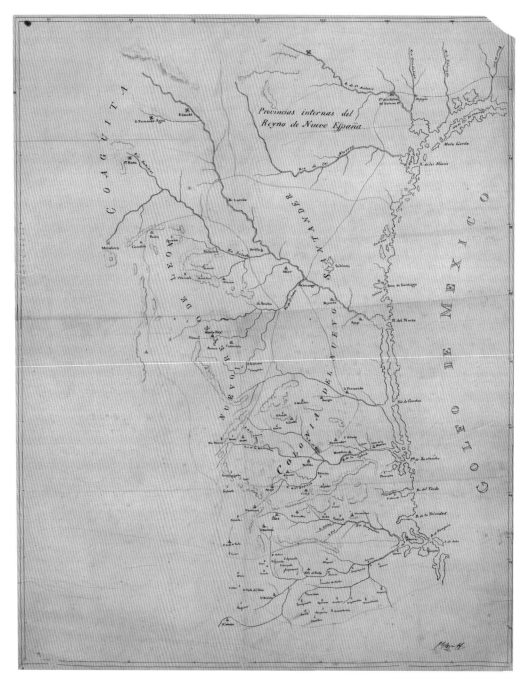

Provincias internas del reyno de Nuevo España, J. G. Bruff (1846).
This charming map depicts the Spanish missions that dotted the Texas landscape and demonstrates the close ties of church and state during both the Spanish and Mexican Eras.

The Texas Revolution

THE MEXICAN CONSTITUTION OF 1824 CREATED the state of Coahuila y Texas, with the capital, Saltillo, in Coahuila and allowed Anglo settlement in Mexico's northernmost province. Catholicism was certified as the national religion, and newcomers were required to take the oath as Mexican citizens and accept the Catholic faith, although the majority of new settlers were Anglo-Saxon Protestants who felt ties with the United States. As for accepting the Catholic faith, the early colonizers coming to Texas were, according to one historian, "lured primarily by economic opportunities. Early American settlers obviously could wear whatever religious garb was required." Although the Constitution of 1824 abolished slavery, a so-called "paper fiction" was allowed to stand, and slavery remained an economic reality with a grim political future. The cultural, religious, and political differences between the Texans, as they increasingly identified as a group, and the Mexican government were strong precursors to rebellion.

The catalyst for the Texas Revolution arrived with new restrictive laws passed by Mexico in April 1830. Following Mexico's independence from Spain in 1822, the government was far from stable. During the period from 1833 to 1855, Mexico lived under some thirty-six presidents. Antonio López de Santa Anna served no less than eleven terms. Passed under Santa Anna's reign, the 1830 law undid the state-oriented freedoms outlined in the Constitution of 1824. Three articles particularly upset the Anglo colonizers: Articles 9 and 11 prohibited any immigration from "nations bordering on this Republic." Article 10 stated, "No change shall be made with respect to the slaves now in the states, but . . . the government of each state shall most strictly en [sic] force the [law] and prevent the further introduction of slaves."

Under the new law any future immigration into Texas would come from south of the Rio Grande. To say Anglo settlers hissed at this law would be a gross understatement. Anglos in Texas had considered themselves Mexican citizens; however, the new law put a chink in the loyalty of the Anglo population, which outnumbered the Mexicans in Texas by four to one (some estimates had it as high as ten to one). Despite the vow of loyalty of Mexican citizenship, the Anglos were an independent lot; they wanted Texas to be a separate and equal state within the Mexican nation. Consultations (a term used by the Texans, thinking the word *convention* too militant) were held over a period of months. In October 1835 members of a consultation resolved to "secure peace if it is to be obtained on constitutional terms, and to prepare for war—if war was inevitable." Stephen Austin wanted peace, and he arrived in Mexico City in July 1833 to present the Texans' grievances to authorities. Again Mexico's central government was in turmoil. Valentín Gómez Farías was acting president, but Santa Anna was standing in the wings, ready to claim the presidential seat. Gómez Farías agreed to revoke Article 11 of the Law of April 6, which halted American immigration into Mexican territory. Politics, however, and a deadly cholera outbreak, delayed any immediate action.

When Austin pushed for action on the petition, heated words were exchanged between the two men. Angry and frustrated by the delay, Austin, his usual clear-minded demeanor failing him, wrote a letter to the *ayuntamiento* (town council) of San Antonio, saying "that the municipality should take the lead in peacefully making preparations for a government distinct from Coahuila." Officials in San Antonio, all Mexicans, viewed the letter as an act of treason and sent it to officials in Saltillo.

Austin was finally able to confer with Santa Anna at the capital. Assured that most of the petition's content was approved (except separation from Coahuila), Austin left Mexico City in good spirits on December 10, 1833. He reached Saltillo in January and was welcomed with imprisonment; authorities used Austin's letter to the San Antonio council as grounds for the arrest. He was returned to Mexico City and held in solitary confinement for several weeks. After some time spent in and out of prison, in July 1835 Austin was released under a general amnesty with an assortment of criminals and other prisoners. Austin returned to Texas a changed man. His time in Mexico and his confinement had convinced him that independence was the only road for Texas.

What is generally considered the first battle of the revolution took place at Gonzales in October 1835. Earlier, when relations between Mexico and the Anglos were much calmer, the latter requested they be given a cannon with which to defend themselves against hostile natives, and Mexico had accommodated the request. But in 1835, when tensions were at the exploding point, Mexico wanted the cannon returned. The settlers refused and displayed a handmade banner emblazoned with the phrase, "COME AND TAKE IT." Lieutenant Francisco de Castañeda, the officer in charge of the Mexican troops, pulled back to San Antonio after a slight skirmish.

General Martín Perfecto de Cos, brother-in-law of Santa Anna, led a force into San Antonio and captured the city. They bivouacked in Mission San Antonio de Valero, what we now call the Alamo. A number of Anglos were anxious to retake the mission and drive Cos back to Mexico, but the main part of the rebel force was ready to fall back and leave the site to the Mexicans. Benjamin Rush Milam cajoled his comrades with the now famous question, "Who will go with old Ben Milam into San Antonio?" (he was forty-eight years old). On December 5, 1835, Milam led three hundred men into San Antonio. On December 9 the Anglos had the Mexican troops penned inside the mission—they had bested their opponents. Aggravated by desertions on his side, Cos surrendered. Old Ben Milam did not get to enjoy the victory; a sniper had killed him on December 7.

In October 1835 an Anglo force led by George M. Collinsworth captured the presidio at Goliad, which was defended by a small Mexican garrison; James W. Fannin was placed in charge of the volunteers at the presidio. Two men, James Grant and Francis W. Johnson, set their eyes on Matamoros, Mexico, on the Rio Grande; the Texas army commander, Sam Houston, was against such a move.

At San Patricio, located in the southwestern corner of today's San Patricio County, General José Urrea, one of Mexico's most able generals, captured or killed most of Grant's and Johnson's men. Following the battle, the Mexicans marched 240 Texans back to Goliad. Santa Anna had decreed that there would be no prisoners taken in the struggle with the Texas rebels—they were to be put to the sword at Goliad, San Antonio, or anywhere they were captured. On Palm Sunday, March 27, 1836, the prisoners were taken out of the presidio, divided into three groups, and marched along three roads: the San Antonio road, Victoria road, and San Patricio road. Their trek was short-lived. Volleys of fire were heard back at the presidio as soldiers massacred their captives.

The first Battle of the Alamo was fought and lost months before the Goliad Massacre took place. Sam Houston, commander of the Texas army, such as it was, ordered the abandonment of the mission and that the place be burned; he knew it was indefensible. Some Texans and Tejanos felt otherwise and prepared to repel Mexican forces to the last man. Aware that there were volunteers in the mission who disagreed with his stand, Houston deferred the matter to Texas governor Henry Smith, and the governor sided with the men in the Alamo. James Clinton Neill was placed in command of the mission garrison, and on January 19, 1836, Colonel James Bowie led a number of volunteers into the mission. On February 3 Lieutenant Colonel William B. Travis reluctantly followed Governor Smith's order and led thirty men into the Alamo. Five days later David Crockett rode into San Antonio with some American volunteers.

Neill left the mission on February 14. He had learned that his family was suffering from a severe but unknown illness, and he was needed in Bastrop, a settlement some 75 miles northeast of San Antonio. Neill left Travis, a regular commissioned officer, a rank bestowed on him by the General Council, in charge of the mission. Some of the volunteers resented this action and called for a vote; Travis and Bowie agreed on a split in command until Neill's return. Travis would command the regulars, Bowie the volunteers. Both "would cosign all orders and correspondence."

Santa Anna crossed the Rio Grande with his forces and marched north. Travis did not believe they could reach San Antonio before March 15, a gross underestimation on the American's part: Santa Anna arrived in the city on February 3. When Santa Anna demanded that the rebels surrender, Travis replied with cannonball. On February 24 Travis assumed command of the Alamo garrison—Bowie had contracted consumption, pneumonia, or some other ailment. Travis wrote his famous letter pleading for help, swearing "Victory or Death." A small contingent of thirty-two men from Gonzales made their way through Mexican lines and entered the Alamo on March 1, 1836.

Santa Anna immediately laid siege to the rebels in the mission. His new hard-line policy was designed to remove the North American presence from Texas, executing or exiling any colonist who had taken part in rebellion and forbidding further emigration from the north.

By March 5 Santa Anna's siege had been in place for twelve days. He ordered an assault on the mission for the following day. His officers recoiled at the order to attack under the circumstances. Surrender was likely. However, Santa Anna would not be put off; he yearned for his pound of flesh. On Sunday, March 6, 1836, around five in the morning, he sent his army, comprising some eighteen hundred (some estimates are as high as four thousand) well-trained troops, from four directions toward the Alamo. The first two assaults were repelled by accurate rifle fire and grapeshot from the cannons of the defenders. The third assault, however, was successful for the Mexican troops; within ninety minutes the Mexican soldiers had taken the Alamo. There were about 189 defenders behind the mission walls—all were killed in the attack.

Santa Anna allowed women and children who survived the battle safe passage through his lines. He wanted the survivors to spread the word of the fate that awaited anyone defying his command. Susanna Dickinson, widow of Captain Almaron Dickinson, accomplished what Santa Anna hoped for: She went directly to Gonzales and informed Houston of the fate of the Alamo. The settlers met her news with fear and panic; they packed what belongings they could and took off for safer ground. With the battle for the Alamo behind him, Santa Anna massed his forces and headed east, chasing what there was of the Texan army. News of his coming and his habit of taking no prisoners created dread among the settlers. Gathering what they could of their possessions, they headed toward the Sabine River and American soil—and safety. In the meantime, Sam Houston was moving his pitiful army east. He knew his small, poorly equipped, poorly trained

army was no match for the more superior Mexican force. Houston had to maneuver his troops to where both armies would meet on equal footing.

"Old Sam" carried an onus on his shoulders. Another Goliad- or Alamo-type defeat would virtually wipe out any further resistance to the Mexican forces. A turnaround by the Texas army had to take place. They crossed the Brazos River on April 14, 1836, and by April 18 the army was at White Oak Bayou. Houston learned that Santa Anna had moved his forces down the west side of the bayou along the San Jacinto River.

At 3:30 in the afternoon of April 21, 1836, the Texans made their move. Santa Anna's troops, apparently unconcerned about the forthcoming battle, were taking their afternoon siesta. The Texans were covered from the Mexicans' view by trees and the elevated ground. Santa Anna had not even bothered posting sentries or any other lookouts.

Amid cries of "Remember the Alamo" and "Remember Goliad," the Texas army of 910 men surprised the Mexicans, and the battle was a complete rout. Revenge was not to be quelled or abated even when Houston implored his men to stop their bloody tirade. The battle lasted only eighteen minutes, but the killing by Texans continued; the troops were set on avenging the Alamo and Goliad and were carried away by the fervor of the moment. The most decisive battle in Texas history was over.

Santa Anna had disappeared. On the day following the battle, Texans found several escapees and escorted them back to the prisoners' compound. None of the Texans really knew what Santa Anna looked like, and they were surprised when the other prisoners began addressing as *el presidente* a wet, bedraggled soldier dressed as a common foot trooper. Only then did they realize the prize they had captured.

Santa Anna was brought before Houston. As arrogant as ever, he demanded that he be treated honorably as a prisoner of war. There were calls among the Texans to execute the man who had brought so much misery, death, and destruction to the settlers. Houston, always thinking ahead, realized that without Santa Anna in the president's seat in Mexico City, there could be no finalization of the war for independence that the Texans had fought so hard to achieve. The Treaties of Velasco, signed by Santa Anna and Texas president Burnet on May 14, 1836, stipulated that hostilities would cease, Mexican troops would be removed from Texas soil, and the Rio Grande would mark the boundary between the Republic of Texas and Mexico.

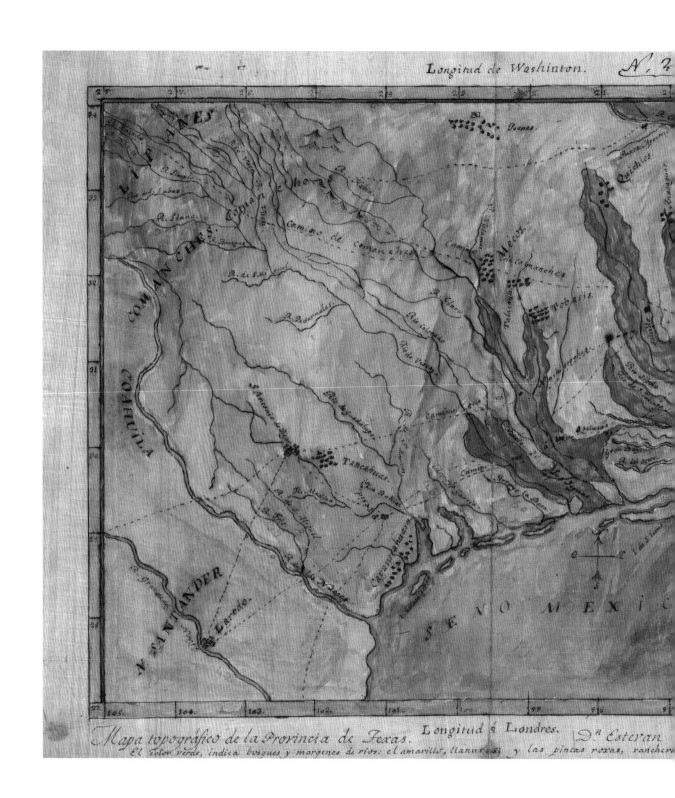

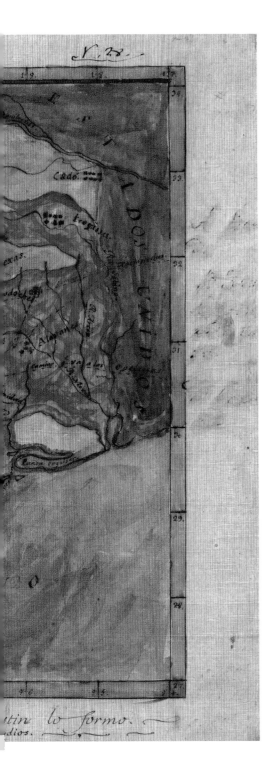

Mapa topográfico de la provincia de Texas, Stephen F. Austin (1822?).

This map, originally drawn by Stephen F. Austin around 1822, denotes an area that he planned to colonize. With what would become the Old Three Hundred, Austin, as *empresario,* settled the colonists on a large section of northern Mexico's province called Texas. The map shows the northeastern section of Mexico and the Rio del Norte (Rio Grande), which would become a point of dispute as to the official boundary line between Mexico and Texas, then between Mexico and the United States.

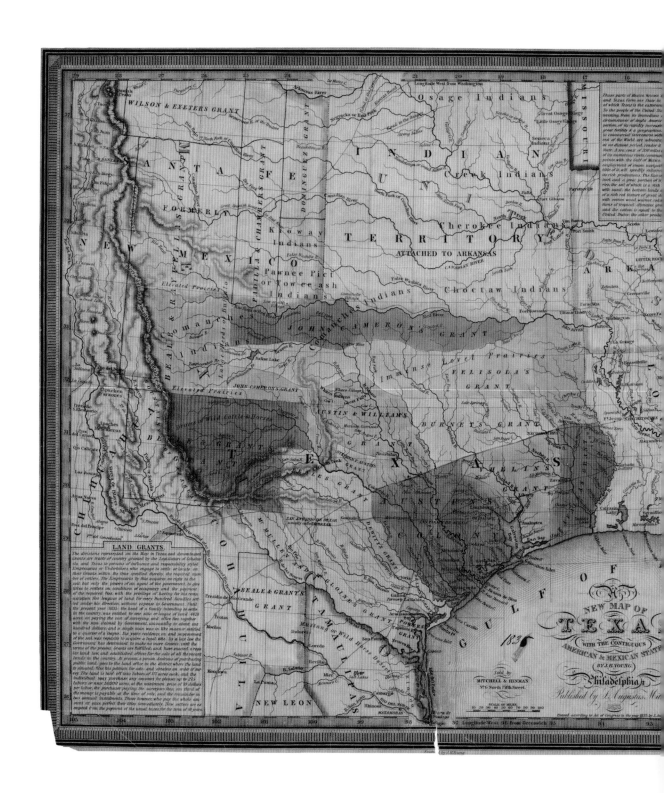

New map of Texas: with the contiguous American & Mexican states, J. H. Young (1835). This map, created and published by S. Augustus Mitchell in 1835, depicts Texas and the bordering American territories of Arkansas (statehood, June 1836) and Indian Territory (Oklahoma). Louisiana, on the eastern border, became a state in April 1812. The Rio Grande flows in a north-to-southeast direction, emptying into the Gulf of Mexico. The states of Mexico that border the Rio Grande are shown.

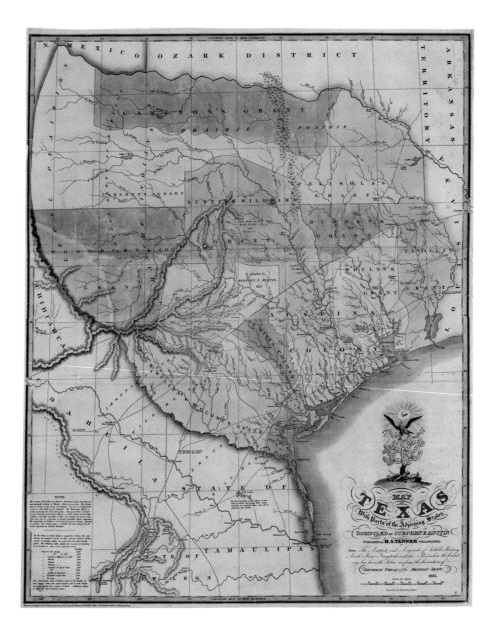

Map of Texas with parts of the adjoining states, compiled by Stephen F. Austin (1837).
This map, published by Henry Schenck Tanner in 1837, reveals how little was known about the size and shape of Texas at the time. The panhandle section is indistinguishable. Arkansas and Louisiana are shown on the eastern part of the map, abutting Texas. Sections of Mexico, including Saltillo and Monterey, are south of the Rio Grande, and Laredo, an entry point from the south, is on the north side of the Rio Grande. Nacogdoches is on the north-eastern point of Texas. Bexar (San Antonio) was the capital of Mexican Texas until the Revolution.

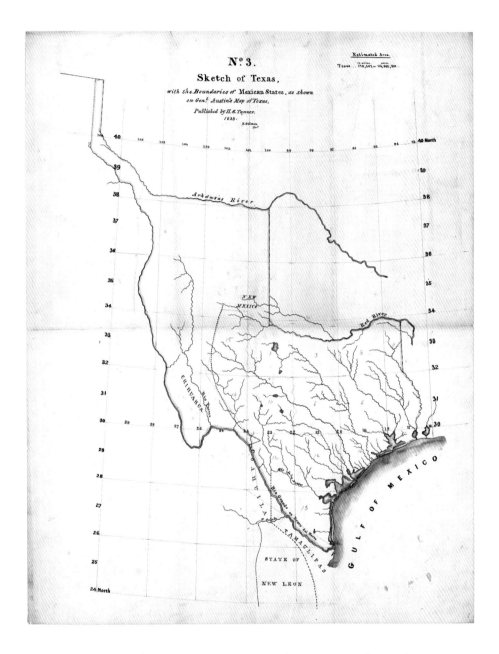

Sketch of Texas with the boundaries of Mexican States as shown on General Austin's map of Texas, E. Gilman (1839).

This map is an early effort to depict the shape and extent of the Texas Republic that was claimed by Texans following the Revolution of 1836. Note that the western boundary follows the Rio Grande into New Mexico territory and the panhandle extends into what would become Colorado.

Map of Texas, William Bollaert (184–?).
This map of Texas, originated by William Bollaert, date unknown, shows an exaggerated version of Texas' boundaries. To the north and east lie the United States territories as known at the time. The map also depicts northern Mexico and the rivers of Texas. The Sabine River, at 94° longitude, came to serve as the official boundary between Louisiana and Texas.

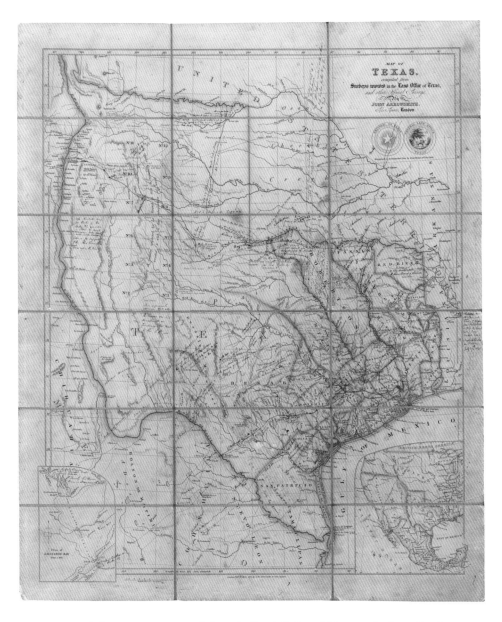

Map of Texas, compiled from surveys recorded in the Land Office of Texas and other official surveys, W. Bollaert (1841).

This map by W. Bollaert, published in the 1840s, is an accurate presentation of Texas, with Indian Territory (Oklahoma) and the state of Arkansas to the north. Louisiana, with the Sabine River separating Texas, is to the east, and territory gained by the United States and still undergoing settlement is to the north. The Gulf of Mexico and some of Mexico's northeastern territories lie south of the Rio Grande.

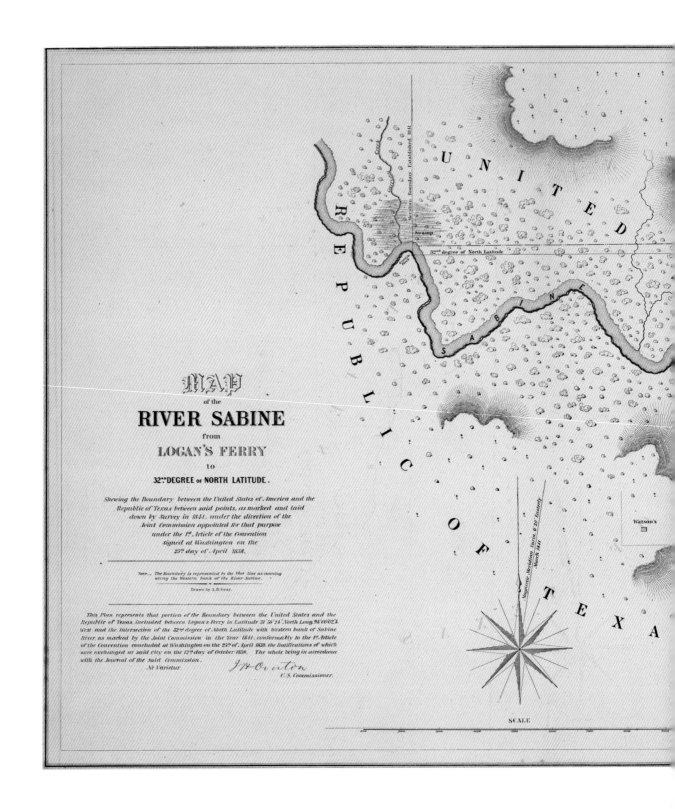

MAP
of the
RIVER SABINE
from
LOGAN'S FERRY
to
32ND DEGREE OF NORTH LATITUDE.

Shewing the Boundary between the United States of America and the
Republic of Texas between said points, as marked and laid
down by Survey in 1841, under the direction of the
Joint Commission appointed for that purpose
under the 1st Article of the Convention
Signed at Washington on the
25th day of April 1838.

Note.. The Boundary is represented by the blue line as running
along the Western bank of the River Sabine.

Drawn by A.B.Gray.

This Plan represents that portion of the Boundary between the United States and the
Republic of Texas, included between Logan's Ferry in Latitude 31°58'24" North Long. 94°00'24"
West, and the Intersection of the 32nd degree of North Latitude with Western bank of Sabine
River, as marked by the Joint Commission in the Year 1841, conformably to the 1st Article
of the Convention concluded at Washington on the 25th of April 1838, the Ratifications of which
were exchanged at said city on the 12th day of October 1838.   The whole being in accordance
with the Journal of the said Commission.
Ne Varietur.
J.H. Overton
U.S. Commissioner.

SCALE

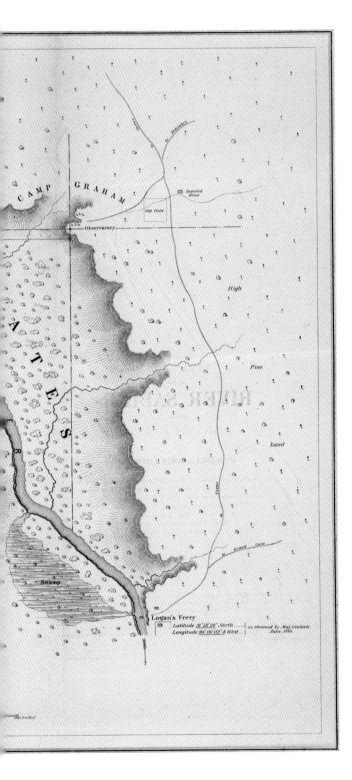

Map of the river Sabine from Logan's Ferry to 32nd degree of north latitude: shewing the boundary between the United States of America and the Republic of Texas between said points, as marked and laid down by survey in 1841, under the direction of the Joint Commission appointed for that purpose under the 1st article of the convention signed at Washington on the 25th day of April 1838, drawn by A. B. Gray (1842?).

This map depicts the U.S./Republic of Texas boundary, the Sabine River. Louisiana is to the east of the Sabine. The Sabine is marked from Logan's Ferry to 32° longitude, which today would place the mark about 75 miles south of the Arkansas border.

Map of Texas and the countries adjacent, William Hemsley Emory (1844).

This map, commissioned by the U.S. Topographical Bureau in 1844, depicts the Republic of Texas and a large part of the Mexican empire spreading to the Pacific Ocean. Much of Mexico, from 20° latitude north and including Baja California, is shown. Louisiana and the Sabine River are east. Some American territory acquired through the Louisiana Purchase lies north of Texas.

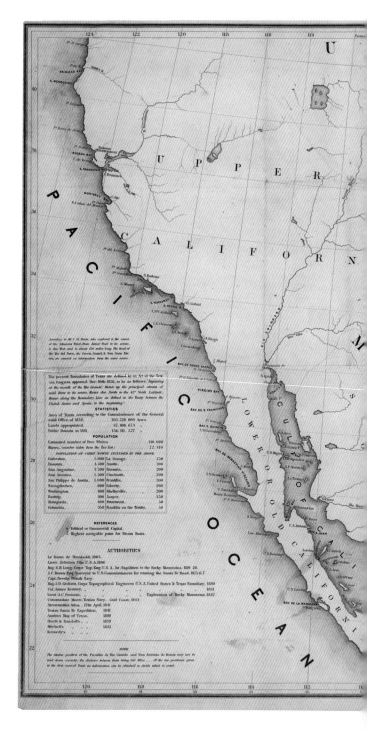

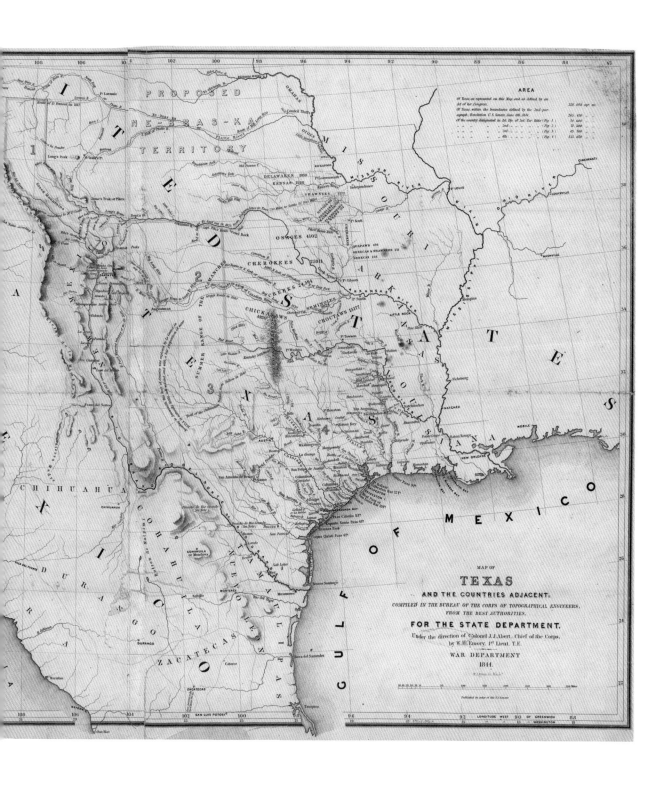

MAP OF

TEXAS

AND THE COUNTRIES ADJACENT,

COMPILED IN THE BUREAU OF THE CORPS OF TOPOGRAPHICAL ENGINEERS,
FROM THE BEST AUTHORITIES.

FOR THE STATE DEPARTMENT.

Under the direction of Colonel J.J.Abert, Chief of the Corps,
by W.H.Emory, 1st Lieut. T.E.

WAR DEPARTMENT
1844.

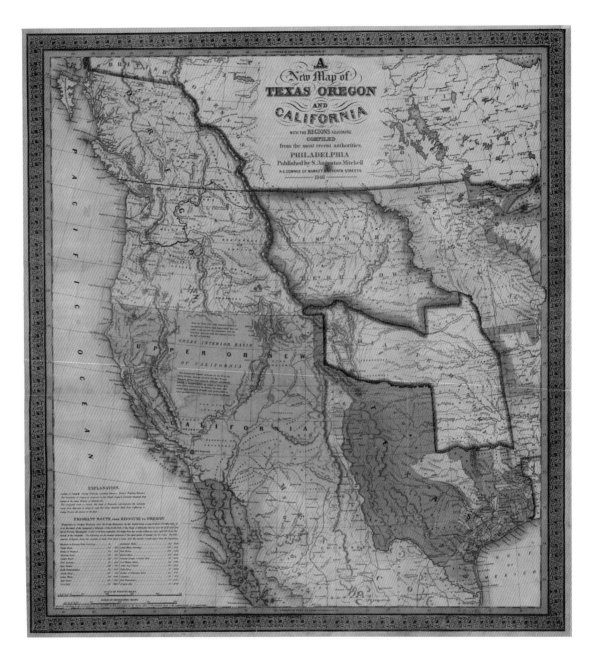

A new map of Texas, Oregon, and California, S. Augustus Mitchell (1846).

This map by S. Augustus Mitchell shows Texas a year or so before being annexed by the United States. Prominent features include California and Oregon, to the Canadian border. The United States and Britain at the time had not settled the northern boundary issue. Much of the future northwestern section of the United States is shown.

Statehood and War

TEXAS GAINED AN UNSTEADY INDEPENDENCE THAT day at San Jacinto, unsteady because authorities in Mexico City claimed the Treaty of Velasco was coerced from Santa Anna while he was a prisoner of the Texans. Mexico looked on Texas as breakaway territory, still part of its empire.

The Texans, however, looked eastward, to statehood and becoming another star in the American flag. A vote held in September 1836 reflected an overwhelming desire on the part of the Texans for annexation by the United States. The proposal was offered to the administration in Washington, but it was rejected, largely due to the fear of war with Mexico. However, slavery also played its part. Texas, if granted admission to the Union, would be a slave state. The antislavery faction became the most dominant drag on the annexation of Texas for the next nine years.

While Sam Houston attempted to placate the Mexicans to the south and the Indians to the west, an antiannexation party gained support within the Republic. Its leader was Mirabeau B. Lamar, who was sworn in as the president of Texas in December 1838. As much as Houston was for annexation, Lamar was just as much opposed. In fact, the new president was the oppo-

site of Houston in many ways. Lamar saw Texas becoming an empire unto itself, building a slave-holding republic stretching all the way to the Pacific Ocean. Lamar and his radical backers threatened to provoke war both to the south, with Mexico, and in Texas, with the Indians.

Lamar's concept of Texas as an independent republic also appealed to some European powers. Texas signed a treaty of recognition with France in 1839; a year later similar treaties were signed with the Netherlands and the British. An important item was not forthcoming from the European countries, however—a loan. Debt continued to pile up for the republic.

Lamar's term ended in 1841, and the war hero, Sam Houston, was once again elected to the president's chair. Houston tried to hold down any military conflict with Mexico. In fact, through a British mediator, Mexico and Texas signed "a general armistice"—not recognition or peace—which went into effect in early 1844. The U.S. Congress was as leery of Texas's expanding to the Pacific Ocean as it was of Britain's gaining a foothold or influence in the republic. On October 16, 1843, President Tyler started renegotiating an annexation agreement, but the United States had treaties it had to observe, and Mexico still had not released Texas from its sphere of influence.

Nevertheless, on April 12, 1844, Texas's representatives signed a treaty with Secretary of State John C. Calhoun whereby the United States would accept Texas as a territory. On June 8 the Senate, with a coalition of antislavery advocates and Southerners who wanted Texas in the Union as a state, voted against the bill. During the presidential campaign of 1844, however, feelings altered. Newspapers editorialized for annexation, people on the street became wrapped up in the idea, and the election of 1844 brought James K. Polk into the White House; Polk was an avowed expansionist. The British and the French, still wanting to gain influence in Texas, had persuaded the Mexican government to recognize Texas independence, but President José Joaquin Herrera realized that Mexico had gotten itself into a precarious position. In May 1845, the Mexican president presented a treaty recognizing Texas's full independence, with the proviso that Texas would not join the American Union. This action was too late; when the Texas Congress met on June 16, it was apparent which treaty the overwhelming majority favored. A formal vote was held, and with only one dissenting vote, the American treaty was accepted.

The United States had never annexed another country before, and authorities were unsure just how to do it, but on December 29, 1845, a vote was taken, the annexation passed, and President Tyler signed the bill admitting Texas to the Union, his last official act before his term ended two days later.

On February 19, 1846, Texas President Anson Jones relinquished his position to the first governor of the state of Texas, James Pinckney Henderson. In an ominous tone Jones said, "The final act in this great drama is now performed; the Republic of Texas is no more."

James K. Polk, who succeeded John Tyler in the presidency in 1846, was an expansionist and a believer in manifest destiny. He knew Mexico had threatened war if the United States annexed Texas, and Polk attempted to placate Mexican authorities by negotiating for the Rio Grande's being the official boundary with Texas. The president also offered to buy northern California from Mexico. Polk's attempts were efforts in futility. Mexico would not agree to cede any territory.

On January 13, 1846, the intransigence of Mexico City caused Polk to order General Zachary Taylor's army, stationed at Corpus Christi, to move some 125 miles south to the Rio Grande. Mexican authorities took this as an act of war. There are disputes over what actually took place next, but consensus is that on April 25 Mexican troops crossed the Rio Grande from Matamoros and attacked an American patrol. This was the only excuse Polk needed. On May 13 he declared war on Mexico for the "shedding of 'American blood upon American soil.'"

A week before Polk's declaration of war, General Taylor's army defeated Mexican forces in two battles, one at Palo Alto and the other at Resaca de la Palma. The battle of Palo Alto took place north of Brownsville and was an indecisive conflict. During the night General Mariano Arista moved his troops to what he believed was a stronger defensive position at Resaca de la Palma, opposite Matamoros. The plan failed because Taylor's troops forced the Mexicans to move south, across the Rio Grande, to a site near Matamoros.

Between five and seven thousand Texans volunteered to fight south of the Rio Grande. The fervor was so high that even Governor Henderson took a leave of absence to command a division of Texas volunteers. Many Texas Ranger units, led by such men as John Coffee Hays and Ben McCulloch, served both General Taylor and General Scott.

The regular troops of the U.S. army looked down on the Rangers regarding their dress and actions. As one cavalryman penned, "Take them altogether, with their uncouth costumes, bearded faces, lean and brawny forms, fierce wild eyes and swaggering manners, they were fit representatives of the outlaws which made up the population of the Lone Star State." Even General Taylor considered the Rangers necessary evils: "Them Texas troops are the damndest troops in the world. . . . We can't do without them in a fight, and we can't do anything with them out of a fight." The Rangers were not above laying heavy and harsh treatment on Mexican guerrillas. As they fought, the memories of the Alamo and Goliad had to cross their minds. They quickly earned the title *les Tejanos diablos,* or the Texas Devils.

The American plan was to instigate a blockade of Mexico and to occupy the northern Mexican states in the hope of bringing the Mexicans to the negotiating table. Taylor, now reinforced by volunteers from the United States, conquered Monterrey in September 1846. Contingents of Texas volunteers, especially Colonel John Coffee Hay and his Texas Mounted Rifles, enhanced the victory.

American victories on the battlefield did nothing to encourage Mexican authorities to negotiate. By right of conquest America could keep all the territory it had captured. There was a feeling in the United States, however, "that the thought of raw aggression did not sit well." A signed, negotiated treaty was much more desirable.

To put pressure on the Mexicans, a large army was formed and led by General Winfield Scott. His object was to march from Veracruz, on Mexico's east coast, to Mexico City. Santa Anna, now back in the presidency in Mexico, sent a force of fifteen thousand against Taylor's forty-six hundred soldiers. At the battle of Buena Vista, on February 22 and 23, 1847, Taylor's troops routed the Mexican force. Much of the success of the battle goes to Texan Major Ben McCulloch and his spy company.

General Scott and his ten-thousand-man army arrived in Mexico on March 9, 1847, and began their march inland. On April 17 and 18 Santa Anna's seventeen-thousand-man army and that of Scott clashed at Cerro Gordo; the Mexican force was practically destroyed. Many of the men with Scott were volunteers whose time was up, and they wanted to go home. This forced Scott to hold his army at Puebla until relief came in the form of Texas Rangers in August. Then Scott moved toward Mexico City. On August 19 and 20, the Americans won victories at Contreras and Churubusco. The Mexican forces were pushed back to the capital, but Santa Anna still would not sue for peace. Scott made a final effort at Molino del Rey on September 8. Determined to bring the Mexican forces to their knees, Scott's troops seized Chapultepec and breached the inner defenses of the city. Santa Anna took off for safer ground.

Mexican authorities knew there was nothing they could do to prevent the Americans from occupying any site in Mexico. Commodore W. Branford Shubrick, commander of the Pacific coast, had taken control of Mazatlán, and secured Baja California and Guaymas. From the Pacific to the Atlantic, Mexico was pretty much at the mercy of American forces.

With Santa Anna absent from Mexico City, the Mexican government was once again in turmoil. Scott and the American envoy, State Department clerk Nicholas Trist, had to cool their heels from September until viable Mexican authorities could be put in place to negotiate a treaty. Trist was to negotiate for Upper and Lower California, New Mexico, and the Rio Grande as boundary between Texas and Mexico. The clerk had the authority to offer Mexican officials $30 million for the territory.

At the outset Mexico would only consider the right of the United States to annex Texas, but Trist stuck to his original instructions, save the removal of Lower California from the negotiations. The Treaty of Guadalupe Hidalgo, signed in February 1848, confirmed the annexation of Texas by the United States and set the Rio Grande as its southern boundary.

At the bargaining table the United States gained Arizona, New Mexico, and California, as well as portions of Utah, Nevada, and Colorado. The United States paid Mexico $15 million for the territory and assumed American citizens' claims against Mexico for $3,750,000. In 1853 the final ceding of land by Mexico was through the Gadsden Purchase, an extension of the Guadalupe Hidalgo treaty. For $10 million the United States gained a direct route from Texas to California, situated south of the Gila River in New Mexico and Arizona. The Treaty of Guadalupe Hidalgo and its extension, the Gadsden Purchase, saw the United States increase in size by 602 million acres.

Texas, nach den besten Quellen entw. u. gez. vom Hauptm. Radefeld (1846).
This map, published in 1846, is similar to the Topographical Bureau presentation of 1844, but there is more relief shown on this map. Mexico runs from about 24º latitude north and encompasses Baja California and its claims west of Texas, including California and New Mexico Territory. Louisiana and the Sabine River are east, and U.S. territory is shown north.

Plan of the ground situated to the north of Matamoras between the Rio Bravo & the Arroyo Colorado, by Luis Berlandier, membro de la commission de geografia militar (1846).

This 1846 map depicts American troop movement and battles during the Mexican-American War. It is a copy of a map taken from the portfolio of General Arista after the battle of May 9, 1846, at Resaca de la Palma.

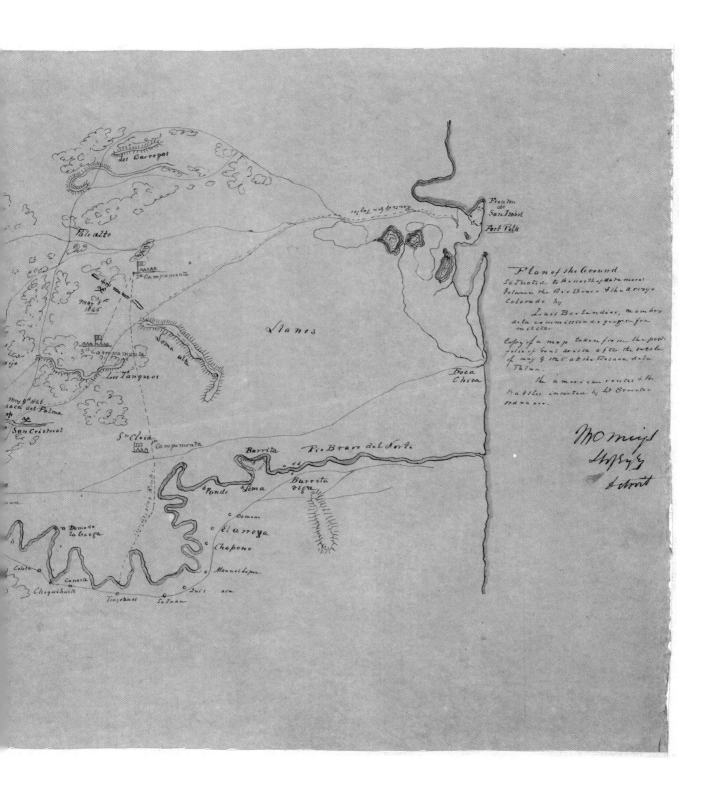

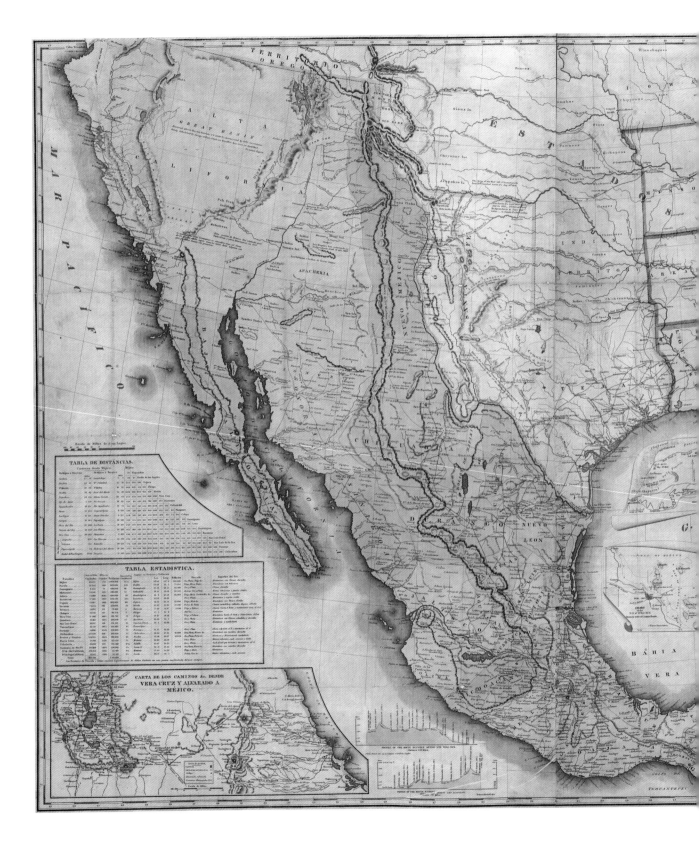

Texas: MAPPING THE LONE STAR STATE THROUGH HISTORY

Mapa de los Estados Unidos de Méjico : segun lo organizado y definido por las varias actas del congreso de dicha república y construido por las mejores autoridades, John Disturnell (1847).
Containing notes and place names in both English and Spanish and the names of battles in the recent war, this 1847 map reflects the still-changing face of the new state of Texas as it relates to its southern neighbors and the rest of the United States.

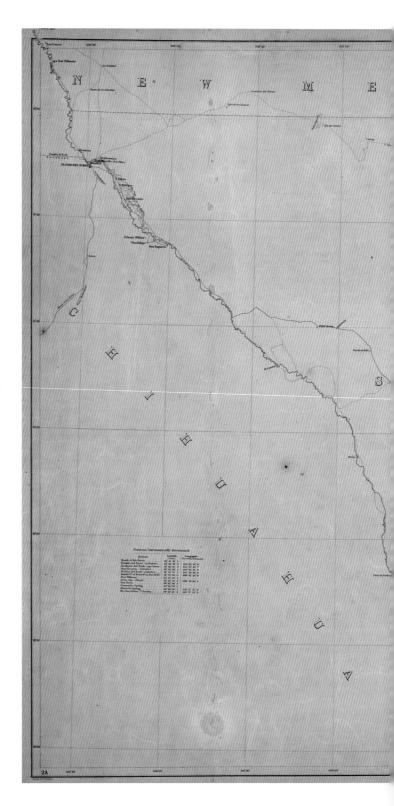

Boundary between the United States and Mexico, William E. Emory (1855).
This map of the new boundary described by the Treaty of Guadalupe Hidalgo, published in 1855 and based on a survey completed two years before, offers an early "official" look at the border.

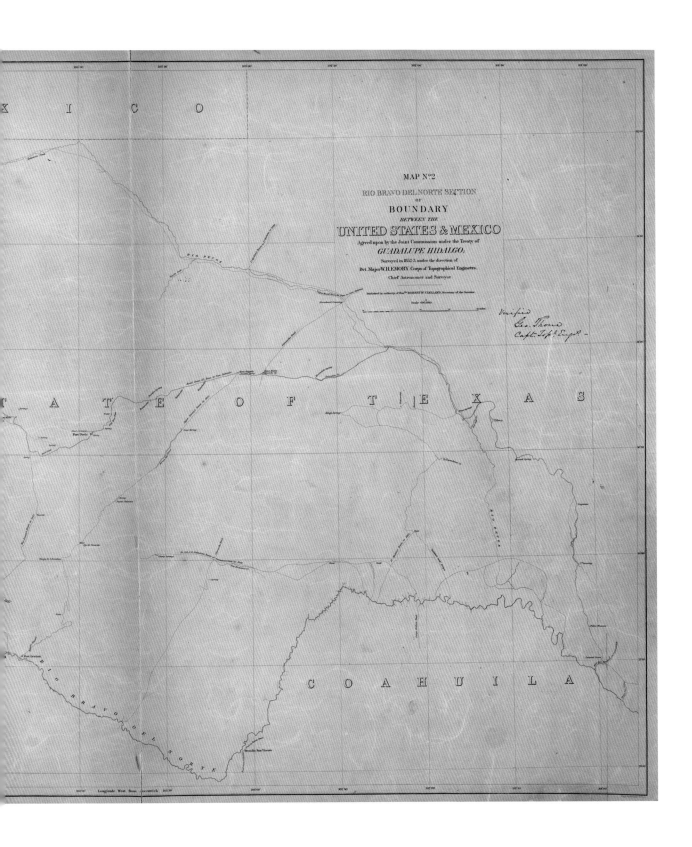

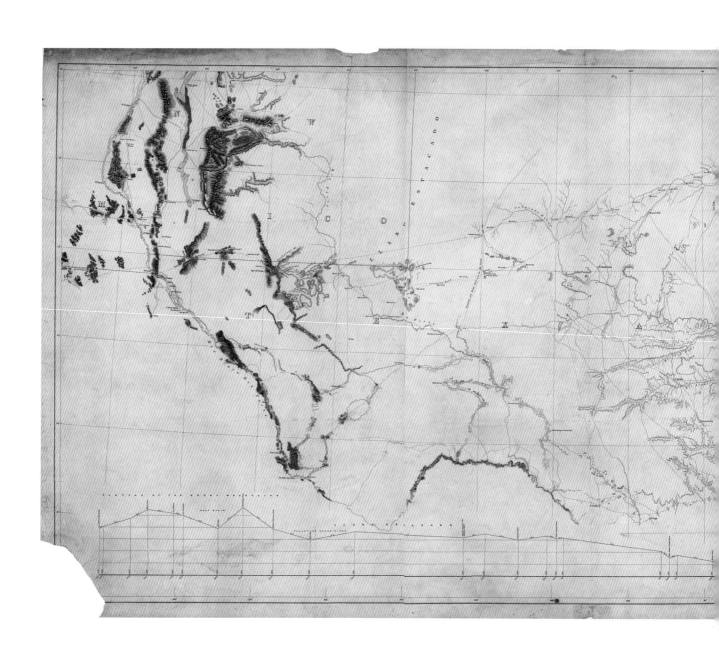

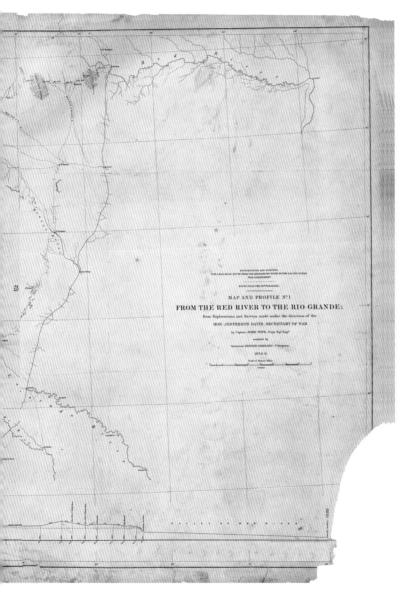

From the Red River to the Rio Grande from explorations and surveys made under the direction of the Hon. Jefferson Davis, by Captain John Pope (1859).

Based on surveys made during soon-to-be Confederate President Jefferson Davis's tenure as secretary of war, this map reveals the ongoing exploration of the vast country acquired from Mexico in 1846.

OFFICE EXPL&S AND SURVEYS
WAR DEP'T.

MAP OF THE
MILITARY DEP'T OF TEXAS.

Being a Section of the Map of the Territory of the U.S.
from the Mississippi River to the Pacific Ocean.
compiled from all the reliable data :
By
Lt. G. K. Warren. T. E.
under the direction of Capt. A. A. Humphreys. T. E.
1859

Scale of Miles

Map of the military dep't of Texas: being a section of the map of the territory of the U.S. from the Mississippi River to the Pacific Ocean compiled from all the reliable data by Lt. G. K. Warren, T.E., under the direction of Capt. A. A. Humphreys, T.E. ; lith. of J. Bien (1859).

The War Department ordered this map in 1859, two years before the onset of the Civil War. It was drawn from data provided by Lieutenant G. K. Warren. The section bordered in red is listed as the military department of Texas. Arkansas and Louisiana border Texas on the east, and New Mexico Territory is shown on the west. North are Indian Territory and a small slice of southern Kansas.

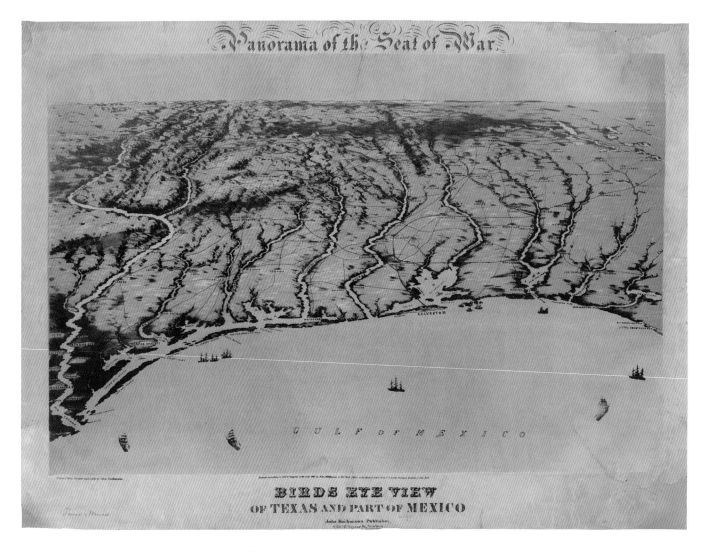

Panorama of the seat of war: bird's eye view of Texas and part of Mexico, drawn from nature and lith. by John Bachmann (1861).

This map by John Bachmann, published in 1861, shows a stretch of Louisiana and Texas along the Gulf of Mexico. The geographic reference is from Little Constance Bay, Vermillon Parish, Louisiana, to the Rio Grande River, Texas. Data accompanying the map state that a section of northern Mexico is included. However, there is little evidence of this feature.

The Civil War

When Abraham Lincoln was elected president of the United States in 1860, many Texans believed the death knell for slavery had sounded. While no more than 25 percent of the families in Texas owned slaves, many of the Anglos who had been settled there through Mexican rule, the republic, and the recent annexation resented the federal government's encroaching on what many considered the rights of states to conduct their own affairs. In addition, the overwhelming majority of the population of the state was Southern by birth or ancestry.

After the election Governor Sam Houston was pushed to convene a convention to discuss secession. Houston was an avowed Unionist; he wanted nothing to do with any secessionist movement. However, when South Carolina seceded from the Union in December 1860 and calls went out for state conventions in Alabama, Florida, Georgia, Louisiana, and Mississippi, Texans were emboldened to step up the pressure to force such a movement in the Lone Star State.

A convention met in Austin on January 28, 1861, and passed the secessionist referendum by a vote of 166 to 8 on February 1. The people passed the bill on February 23 by a vote of 46,153 to 14,747. The following month the convention reassembled, declared Texas no longer in the Union, and voted to join the other breakaway states in the Confederate States of America. Houston declined to recognize the actions of the convention and refused to take an oath of allegiance to the new government. The convention declared the office of governor vacant and placed Lieutenant Governor Edward Clark in the governor's chair.

President Lincoln offered to send federal troops to Texas to support Houston should he choose to defy the action of the convention, but Houston had no desire to see a civil war in his state and declined the president's offer. The hero of San Jacinto packed his personal belongings and retired to his home in Huntsville, Alabama. He died at home on July 26, 1863, at age seventy.

Few Civil War battles took place on Texas soil, though Galveston came under heavy attack early in the conflict. On October 4, 1862, a Union fleet attacked the Confederate guard at Galveston and took control of the city. Less than three months later, on New Year's Day, 1863, Texas troops commanded by General John Bankhead Magruder used a combination of Texas land

and water forces to retake the island. In September 1863 the Union attempted another assault on Galveston, but the effort failed.

General Nathaniel P. Banks planned a Union attack on Texas through Sabine Pass. In September 1863 he sent five thousand troops by transports up the Sabine River, supported by four gunboats. The Unionists' goal was to use Sabine Pass to capture Beaumont and possibly move on to Houston. A small detachment of Confederate soldiers, under command of Lieutenant Richard Dowling, a saloonkeeper with some artillery experience, not only repelled the invasion but in less than an hour had captured two of the gunboats and sent the other two scurrying back to safety. Dowling's men killed or captured 350 federal troops. Confederate President Jefferson Davis called the actions of Dowling and his men "one of the most brilliant and heroic achievements in the history of this war."

In November 1863 seven thousand Union troops commanded by General Banks captured Rio Grande City and Corpus Christi. They also conquered Brownsville, which temporarily severed the supply line between Texas and Mexico. A major Union offensive was in the offing for the spring of 1864, and most of Banks's troops were ordered to Louisiana to participate. With much of the Union force now depleted, John S. Ford and troops under his command were able to reoccupy the sites lost to the North. By the end of the Civil War, the only part of Texas in Union control was Brazos Island, south of Padre Island.

In August 1862 a group of some sixty-five Union sympathizers led by Fritz Tegener attempted to reach Mexico. Their intentions seemed mixed: Some wanted to get to safety; others wanted to join up with Union forces. They were caught by Confederate troops led by Lieutenant C. D. McRae at the Nueces River. Thirty-five of the dissidents were killed and several wounded. Residents of the south-central county of Gillespie witnessed the hanging of fifty Union supporters.

The Red River counties of Cooke and Grayson, where opposition was strongest, were the sites of probably the greatest injustice during the period. A "citizens' court" at Gainesville arrested and tried 150 people for suspected Unionist activities. Thirty-nine were executed after either confessing or being convicted by the "court" for their activities.

About twenty-five hundred Tejanos fought for the Confederacy, probably intimidated into doing so; their desertion rates were exceedingly high. Most Tejanos looked on the Civil War as an opportunity to avenge hatreds that had been festering since the Revolution of 1836, when they felt they had been victims of the Anglos.

The last battle of the war fought on Texas soil was at Palmito Hill, north of Brownsville, on May 13, 1865, a month and four days after General Lee's surrender at Appomattox Courthouse. Though Texas had an opportunity to reenter the Union and avoid the degradation of Reconstruction in exchange for troops to help fight the French in Mexico, those overtures were rejected. Texas was placed under martial law on June 19, 1865, the same day General Gordon Granger read the Emancipation Proclamation for the first time in Texas. Lincoln's act freed some quarter million slaves in the state. In 1979 Governor William P. Clements Jr. signed a bill into law establishing "Juneteenth" as a state holiday.

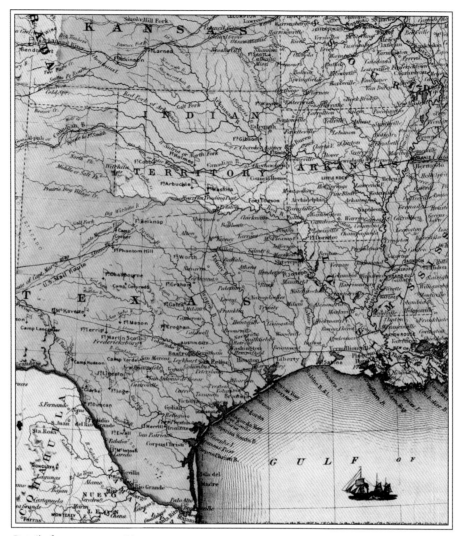

Detail of map on page 56.

Map of Texas, showing the line of the Texas and New Orleans Rail Road, and its connections in the U.S. and adjacent territories, A. M. Gentry (1860). The map of the Texas area by A. M. Gentry, published in 1860, shows the railroad partially built and running from New Orleans almost in a straight line into Texas. The Civil War halted all construction in Texas and throughout the South; once the war was over, construction started up again. Sections of Mexico to the south are shown, as well as parts of Arkansas, Louisiana, and other nearby states.

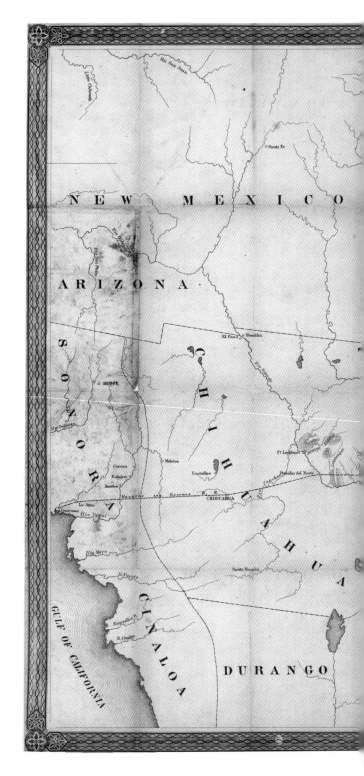

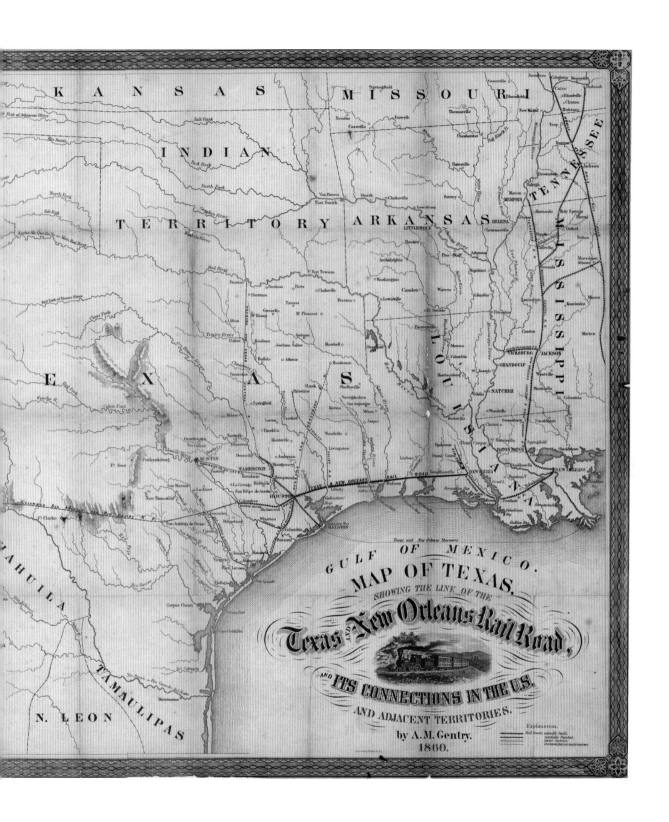

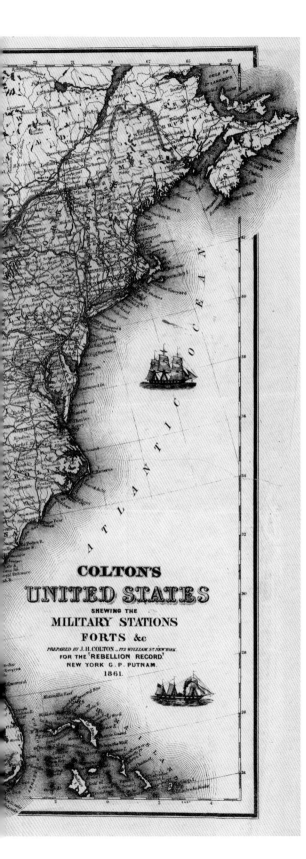

Colton's United States shewing the military stations, forts, &c Prepared for the "Rebellion Record," J. H. Colton (1861).
This map by J. H. Colton, published in 1861 by G. P. Putnam, shows the eastern portion of the United States from about 103° longitude north to Canada. A very small section of northeast Mexico is shown south of the Rio Grande. Data accompanying the map annotates it as "shewing [sic] the military stations, forts, &c . . . for the 'Rebellion Record.'"

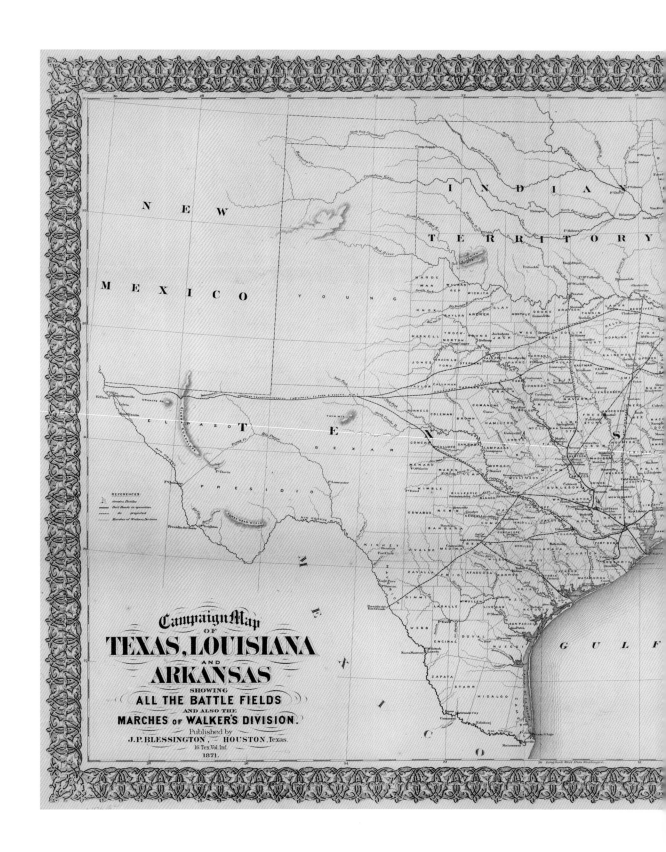

Campaign map of Texas, Louisiana and Arkansas, showing all the battle fields and also the marches of Walker's Division. [1861–65] Entered according to Act of Congress in the year 1871 by E. H. Cushing. Engraved, printed and manufactured by G. W. & C. B. Colton & Co., New York (1871).

This 1871 map by E. H. Cushing shows Texas, Arkansas, and Louisiana during the Civil War. The map indicates regional battlefields. It also reflects the engagements of Texas general John G. Walker in Louisiana. He and his forces, called the "Greyhound Division" because they were able to cover great distances in a short period of time, disrupted Union forces in several battles, thus probably preventing Texas from suffering more invasions by Northern troops.

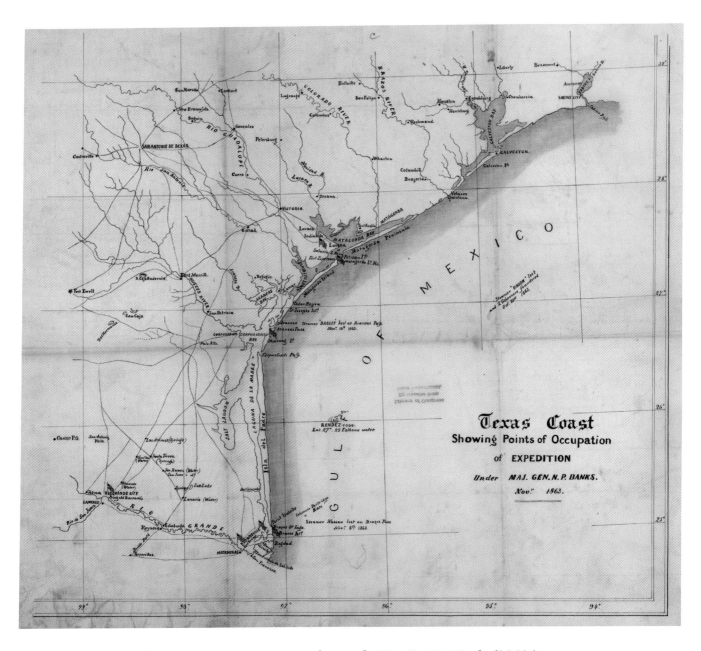

Texas Coast showing points of occupation of expedition under Maj. Gen. N. P. Banks (1863?).

This map, created in 1863, depicts the Texas coast. It shows rivers, roads, and occupation sites by Union forces. General N. P. Banks attempted two invasions of Texas but was defeated in both. In 1863 his forces tried to enter Texas via Sabine Pass and were handed an embarrassing defeat. In 1864 Banks was again battered, this time by a much smaller Confederate force at Mansfield, Louisiana.

The Postwar Era

MORE THAN FIFTY THOUSAND UNION SOLDIERS marched into Texas at the end of the Civil War to begin the process of "reconstructing" the former Confederate state into the Union. Republican Andrew J. Hamilton was appointed provisional governor of Texas and charged with the task of calling a convention to nullify the act of secession and abolish slavery in the state. Once these were accomplished, the voters would choose a governor, a legislature, and other state officials. Once the legislature ratified the so-called "reconstruction" amendments to the U.S. Constitution, the state would be readmitted to the Union.

During the convention Unionists attempted to have the secession declared null and void from the beginning. The attempt failed to pass. The delegates did renounce the right of secession but refused to accept that the action was wrong from the beginning. They agreed to the abolition of slavery but refused to recognize black suffrage. There were simply too many former breakaway advocates dominating the state legislature; they saw to it that the Fourteenth and Fifteenth Amendments were not ratified and enacted "black codes," laws designed to control the newly freed black population. Republicans in the North and Unionists in Texas viewed this act as nothing more than slavery in disguise.

When on March 2, 1867, the U.S. Congress divided the South into military districts, Texas was placed in the Fifth Military District. The following two years of martial law had their intended effect. In a state election held in December 1869, Edmund J. Davis was elected governor, and members of the Twelfth Legislature met in Austin and passed the Fourteenth and Fifteenth Amendments in quick order. A little more than two months later, on March 30, 1870, President Grant put his signature to the act that "readmitted Texas to the Union and ended Congressional Reconstruction."

Readmitting Texas to the federal Union, however, did not settle Texas's problems. Crime was rampant in the northeast section of the state, along the Red River, and in the Big Thickets of East Texas. Much of the violence was racially or politically inspired, aimed at free blacks and federal soldiers. To fight the violence the legislature established the state police and a militia. While the state police seemed to accomplish their mission, the organization received noticeable criticism, both warranted and unwarranted from citizens. The militia, used sparingly, was also resented.

On the Texas frontier the "Indian question" remained a hot-button issue. There had been many massacres on both sides of the Indian-settler fights. On May 18, 1871, about 150 Indians attacked a large wagon train at Salt Creek, situated between Jacksboro and Fort Griffin. The Salt Creek slaughter, led by war chiefs Santana and Big Tree, was one of the most atrocious on record. The Indians killed seven men; five others managed to avoid death or capture. One of them, named Brazeal, made it to Jacksboro even though he was severely wounded. General William T. Sherman interviewed Brazeal at Fort Richardson, near Jacksboro. The appearance of the wounded man, and the story he told of the atrocity of the Indian attack, changed Sherman's views regarding American Indian depredations. His attitude further hardened when he read the official army report by troops who found the remains of the raid: "The horribly, bloody, mutilated, fly-covered bodies of the teamsters . . . the body of Sam Elliott, . . . described as found hung face-down over a burnt-out fire, his tongue cut out and his body crisped, changed Sherman's mind."

The general ordered Colonel Ranald S. Mackenzie to take to the field with four companies of the Fourth Cavalry. Mackenzie had a free hand, given discreetly, to settle the Indian problem in Texas. Most of the Indians were forced into Palo Duro Canyon, near Amarillo, where Mackenzie shot their horses. A Plains Indian without his horse is a defenseless creature. By 1875 the last of the great American Indian tribes in Texas were either broken up or relegated to reservations.

When in 1872 Democrats gained control of the Texas House, the legislature, aided by the old stalwart Republicans now working in tandem with the Democrats, set about undoing much of the accomplishments of Reconstruction, from abandoning education reform to abolishing the state police and militia. In the election of December 1873, Democrat Richard Coke won the governorship, marking the beginning of a string of Democratic governorships that continued for 106 years, until Republican William Clements broke the string in 1979.

Reconstruction had allowed the rise of black social and economic units. Although not fully integrated into the state's social structure, former slaves had developed their own society of schools and churches and to some extent their own economy. In 1870 there were an estimated quarter million blacks in Texas, compared to some twenty-three thousand Mexican-Americans, who also lived predominantly in their own society, mostly in the region along the Rio Grande.

The year 1870 saw the rise of a few ten-thousand-plus-populated cities. Galveston was the largest and most influential, with a population exceeding thirteen thousand. San Antonio was second with more than twelve thousand people, and both Houston and Austin were on the cusp of becoming metropolitan centers. Also at this time in Texas history, there were an estimated four million head of longhorn cattle that had been allowed to roam free and multiply on the open range. When veterans of the Civil War returned home, many were hired as cowboys, to "rope, tie, and brand 'em." Cattle worth four dollars in Texas brought ten times that amount up north. In 1866 about 260,000 cattle were prodded to market over the various trails from Texas to rail centers in Kansas and Missouri. In the spring of 1871, the number jumped to 700,000, the largest count for a single year's drive. Between 1865 and 1880 some five million cattle were driven north on the trail drives. By 1885, though, the railroad had reached Texas, and the need for trail drives was over; instead cattle were transported north by train.

Postwar Texas was primarily a rural state. Towns were rare and sparsely populated; they catered to people from the outlying sections who came into the city to buy dry goods and limited amounts of foodstuffs. One of the more popular places of business was the drugstore, where patent medicines for various ailments were increasingly available and did little good and some harm. Doctors were in short supply, and those who were available were little more than quacks.

The saloon underwent a change from a place of whiskey barrels and a board to an elegant place of business. The gin mills became social and political conduits for all variety of opinions and the setting for many gunfights. To contravene the saloons, there arose in the towns churches of various faiths. Prominent among these were the Baptist, Episcopalian, Lutheran, Methodist, Presbyterian, and Roman Catholic. An estimate in 1870 put the number of churches at 843, spread across Texas and claiming memberships of about two hundred thousand.

By the year 1890 the last great rush of migration to Texas had taken place. In 1870 there were about 818,175 people in Texas, of which 250,000 were black. Fifteen years later the population had skyrocketed to 2,245,527. The percentage of blacks dropped tremendously, since the new arrivals did not bring any slaves with them.

Cotton was a king crop. In 1886 the state produced more than a million and a half bales of the white stuff, compared with about one-third that amount in 1874. But cotton, like the water supply and soil of Texas, was fickle. By 1898 cotton was selling for as little as five cents per pound, compared to the thirty-one cents it brought in 1865.

This was also the era of the big ranches. The enormous King Ranch had developed in the 1850s. Postwar giants in West Texas and the panhandle included the Matador, Hansford Company, and Espula (Spur). The biggest to come out of the region was the XIT Ranch. Proceeds from the sale of state land to the XIT conglomerate were used to construct the capitol building in Austin.

It would be impossible for any Texan, except perhaps a few farsighted individuals, to know what lay ahead for the state at the turn of the century. The year 1900 would inaugurate a period of vast changes to the state—some good, some bad.

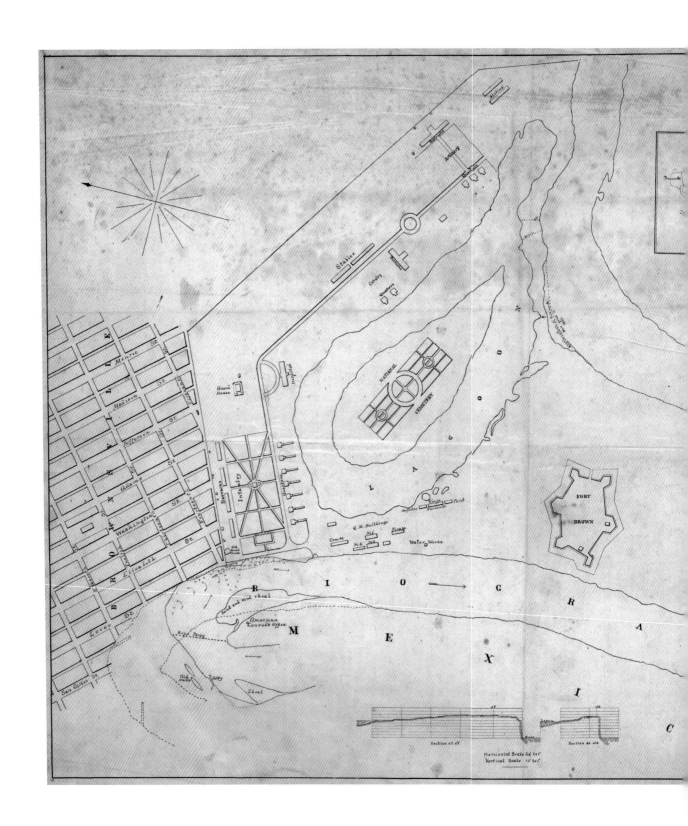

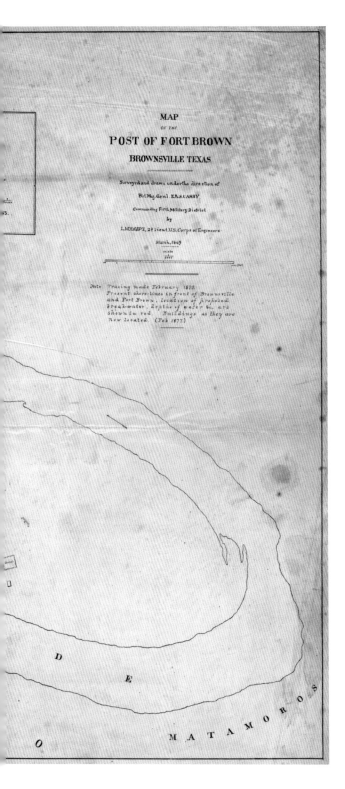

Map of the post of Fort Brown, Brownsville, Texas, surveyed and drawn under the direction of B'vt Maj. Genl. E. R. S. Canby, commanding fifth military district by L. M. Haupt, 2nd Lieut. U.S. Corp. of Engineers, March 1869 (1877).

This map, sketched in March 1869 by 2nd Lieutenant L. M. Haupt, U.S. Corps of Engineers, shows north to the left. The site was known as Fort Texas when constructed by General Zachary Taylor in March 1846. It was renamed for Major Jacob Brown, who was killed during bombing by Mexican forces in Matamoros, Mexico, across the river from the fort. During the Civil War the fort changed hands several times between federal and Confederate troops. The fort served a variety of usages until officially deactivated in 1945.

Schönberg's map of Texas, Schönberg & Co. (1866).
This 1866 map shows the post–Civil War state of Texas as it would have appeared during the Reconstruction years. Counties were forming, communities were growing, and the march of troops into the state would bring stability and new authority to the region as it shaped its identity for the future.

SCHÖNBERG'S
MAP OF
TEXAS.

Scale of English Statute Miles

Colton's new map of the state of Texas : the Indian Territory and adjoining portions of New Mexico, Louisiana, and Arkansas, compiled from the official county maps of the General Land Office, the personal reconnaisances and geological explorations of Prof. A. R. Roessler, the surveys of the Mexican Boundary Commission, U.S. Coast Surveys, U.S. General Land Office, the various Rail Road Cos., information furnished by Mr. Pressler, and other authentic materials by G. Woolworth Colton (1872).

This map was drawn by G. Woolworth Colton and published in 1872. It defines the Texas boundaries with New Mexico Territory, Indian Territory (Oklahoma), Arkansas, and Louisiana. The Texas depiction shows the wide-open High Plains region beginning at 100° longitude, 37° latitude. It lays out Texas's border along the Gulf of Mexico, as well as northern Mexico.

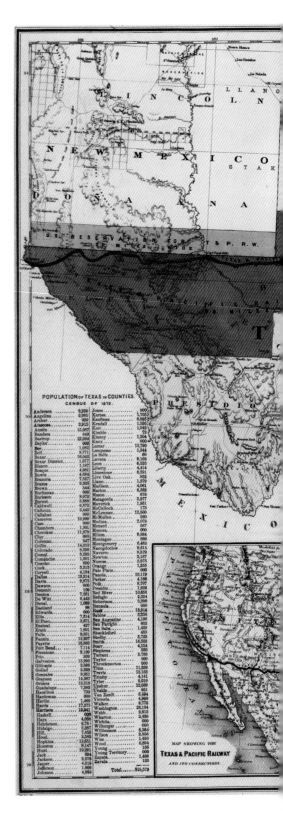

Map of the state of Texas showing the line and lands of the Texas and Pacific Railway reserved and donated by the State of Texas, G. W. & C. B. Colton & Co. (1873).

This 1873 map of Texas, drawn by G. W. & C. B. Colton & Co., reflects the expansion of the railroad once the Civil War was over. The red area marks the Texas and Pacific Railway line, as well as land ceded by the state. The insert shows the line projection all the way to the Pacific Ocean. This map was drawn after the legislature overrode the governor's veto of a railroad expansion bill.

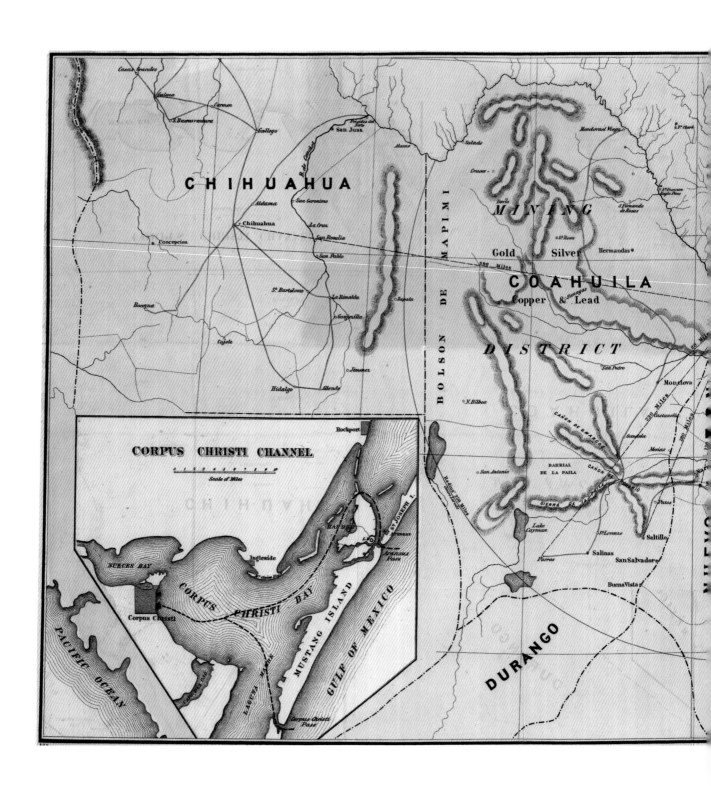

CHIHUAHUA

CORPUS CHRISTI CHANNEL

Scale of Miles

BOLSON DE MAPIMI

MINING

Gold Silver

COAHUILA

Copper & Lead

DISTRICT

DURANGO

Texas: MAPPING THE LONE STAR STATE THROUGH HISTORY

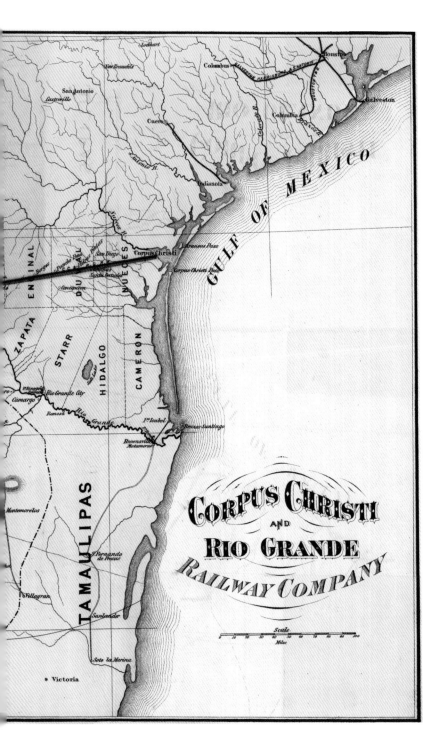

Corpus Christi and Rio Grande Railway Company [map showing the proposed railroad between Laredo and Corpus Christi and its connections with Mexico], Julius Bien (1874).

This 1874 map, drawn by Julius Bien, shows the projected route of the Corpus Christi and Rio Grande Railroad. On January 1, 1878, the railway company opened 25 miles from Corpus Christi to Banquete. The following year the line was extended 27 miles from Banquete to San Diego. Richard King and Mifflin Kenedy (of Santa Gertrudis Ranch) supported the line's continuation; the line was renamed Texas Mexico Railway Company in June 1881.

Texas and Pacific Railway and its connections, G. W. & C. B. Colton & Co. (1876).

G. W. & C. B. Colton & Co. published this 1876 map of the route of the Texas Pacific Railway. On May 2, 1872, Congress changed the name to Texas and Pacific Railway Company. The T&PRC was granted authority to construct a railroad from Marshall, Texas, to San Diego, California. On October 15, 1976, the T&PRC merged with the Missouri Pacific Railway.

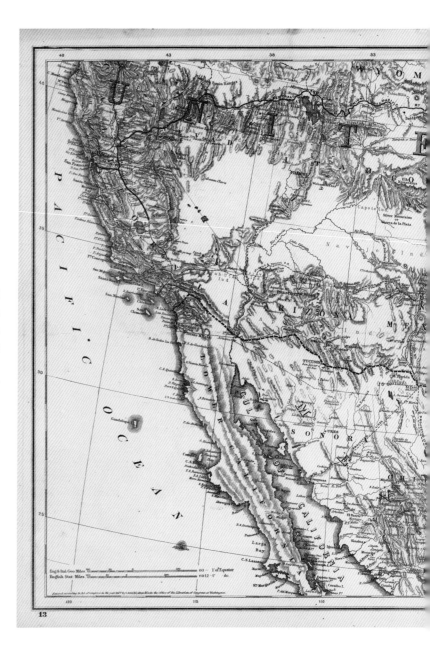

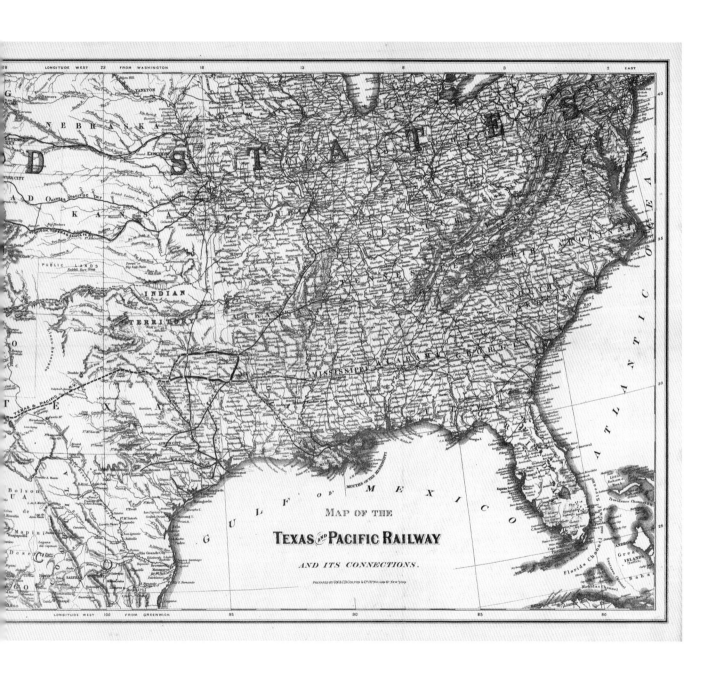

MAP OF THE

TEXAS AND PACIFIC RAILWAY

AND ITS CONNECTIONS.

PREPARED BY G.W.&C.B.COLTON & C.º 172 WILLIAM St. New York.

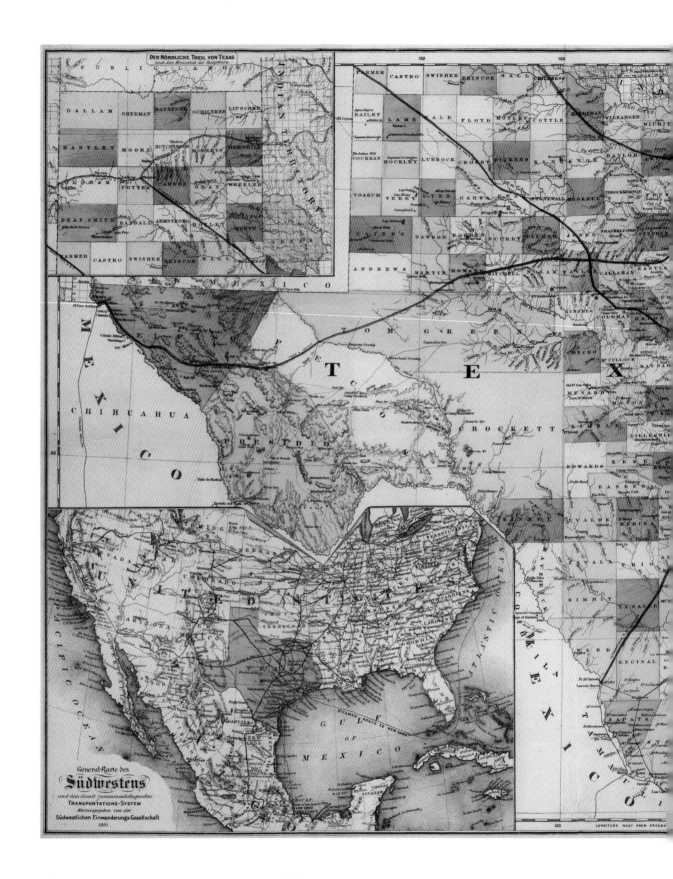

Texas: MAPPING THE LONE STAR STATE THROUGH HISTORY

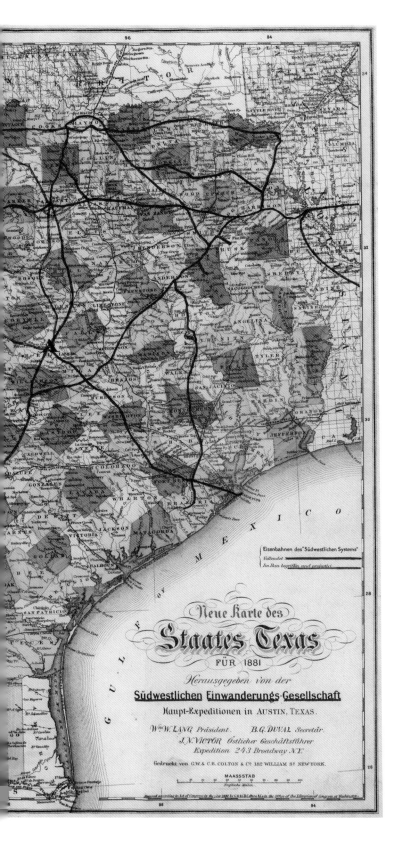

Neue Karte de Staates Texas, G. W. & C. B. Colton & Co. (1881).
G. W. & C. B. Colton & Co. created and published this map in 1881. The counties shown in the inset are part of the northwestern section of the state known as the High Plains. With some exceptions the counties shown in the inset were created from the Bexar District around 1876.

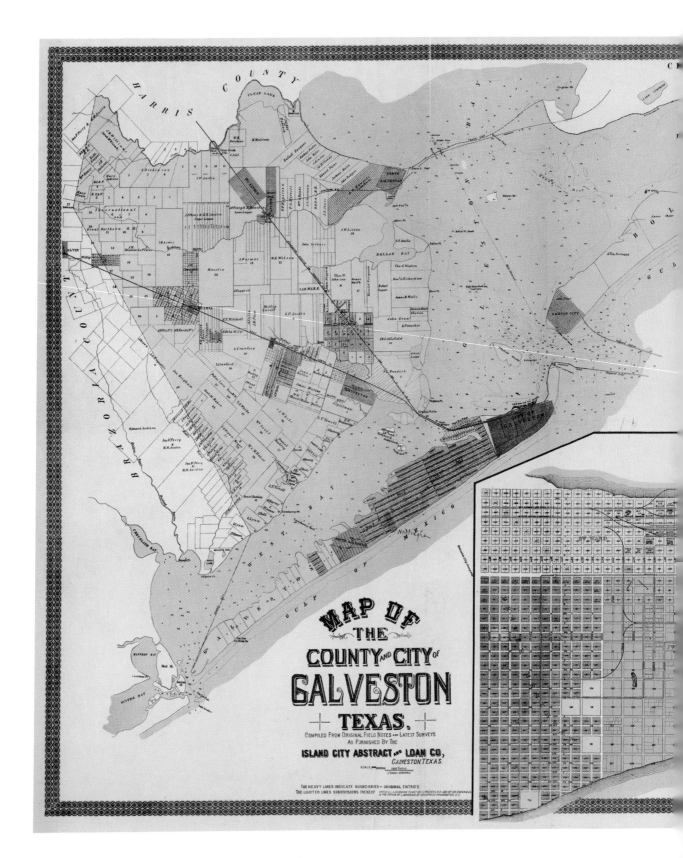

MAP OF THE COUNTY AND CITY OF GALVESTON TEXAS.

COMPILED FROM ORIGINAL FIELD NOTES AND LATEST SURVEYS
AS FURNISHED BY THE

ISLAND CITY ABSTRACT AND LOAN CO,
GALVESTON, TEXAS.

THE HEAVY LINES INDICATE BOUNDARIES OF ORIGINAL ENTRIES
THE LIGHTER LINES SUBDIVISIONS THEREOF

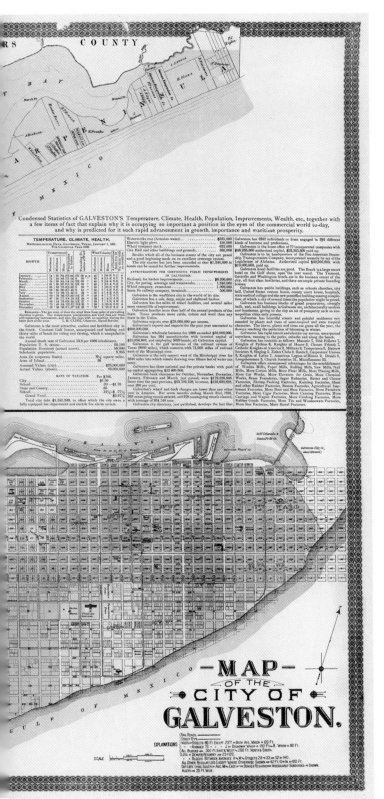

Map of the county and city of Galveston, Texas, compiled from original field notes and latest surveys, Island City Abstract and Loan Co. (1891).

The pirate Jean Lafitte moved to Galveston Island in 1817 and established a town he christened Campeachy. By 1870 the town, renamed Galveston, had a population of twelve thousand, which jumped to twenty-two thousand by 1881. It was the center for cotton exports, home to fabulous mansions, and an insurance and banking center.

Dallas, Texas. With the projected river and navigation improvements viewed from above the sister city of Oak Cliff, Paul Giraud (1892).
The Dallas Lith. Co. published this map in 1892. With the arrival of the railroads, Dallas grew in population from three thousand in 1870, to thirty-eight thousand in 1890, when it was the largest city in Texas. It also became a center for banking and insurance. The city acquired its first telephones in 1881 and electricity the following year. In 1903 Dallas annexed Oak Cliff.

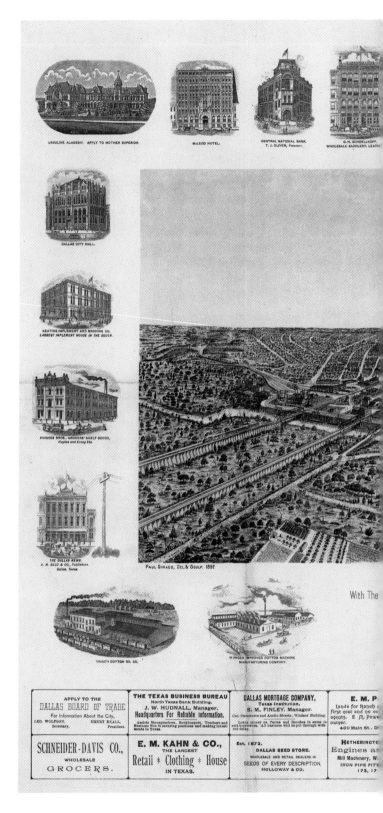

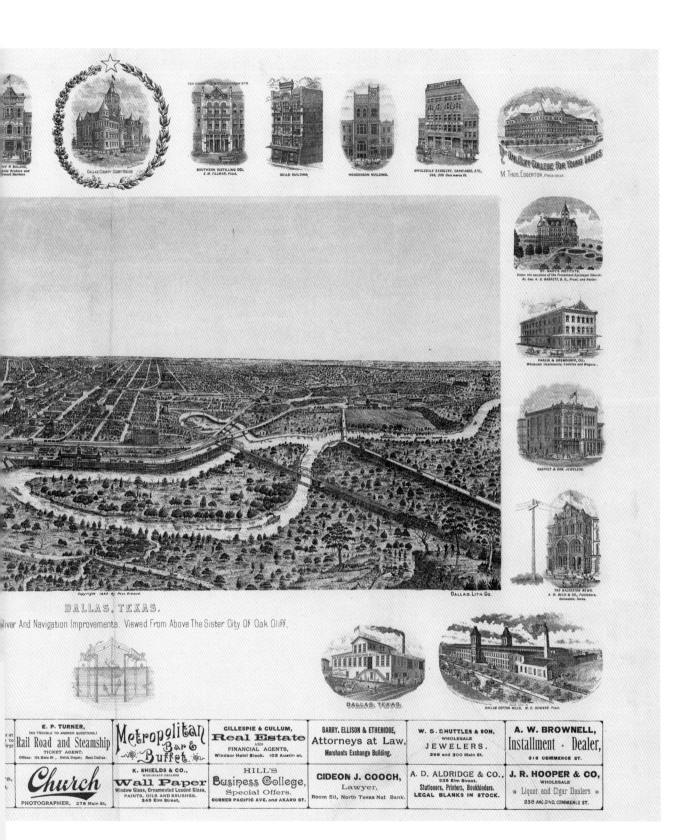

Southern Distilling Co., E. H. Tillman, Prest.

Guild Building.

Henderson Building.

Wholesale Saddlery, Carriages, Etc., 248, 250 Commerce St.

Oak Cliff College For Young Ladies. M. Thos. Edgerton, President.

Dallas County Court House.

St. Mary's Institute. Under the auspices of the Protestant Episcopal Church. Rt. Rev. A. C. Garrett, D. D., Prest. and Rector.

Parlin & Orendorff, Co. Wholesale Implements, Vehicles and Wagons.

Knepfly & Son, Jewelers.

The Galveston News. A. H. Belo & Co., Publishers, Galveston, Texas.

Copyright 1892 by Paul Giraud.

DALLAS, TEXAS.

River And Navigation Improvements. Viewed From Above The Sister City Of Oak Cliff.

Dallas Lith. Co.

DALLAS, TEXAS.

Dallas Cotton Mills, W. C. Howard, Prest.

BAYLOR UNIVERSITY.

BOULEVARD ADDITION.
GATES, SCHUMACHER, MEYERHOEFER & CO.

PACIFIC HOTEL.
WACO, TEXAS.
O. W. BUDE, PROPRIETOR.

INSIDE VIEW OF
H. G. RISHER & CO.
PRESCRIPTION DRUG STORE.
305 SOUTH 8TH STREET.
WACO, TEXAS.

BUILDING OF THE PROVIDENT SAVINGS LIFE ASSURANCE
SOCIETY OF NEW YORK.
R. S. PARROTT, MANAGER TEXAS, ARKANSAS and PACIFIC SLOPE.
WACO, TEXAS.

M. L. WINA...

BUSINESS DIRECTORY.

A. Post Office and N. S. Court House.
B. Court House.
C. City Hall.
D. Pacific Hall.
E. Hotel Royal.
F. Central High School.
G. "The Daily News."
H. "The Day."
I. Provident Saving Life Assurance Society.
J. Waco University.
K. Methodist Female College.
L. New Methodist Female College.
M. City Hospital.
N. Electric Power House.

O. Electric Power House.
P. Cameron Roller Mills.
Q. Grain Elevator.
R. Hubly & German Roller Mills.
S. Gas Works.
T. Padgetts Park Theatre.
U. Natatorium.
V. Waco Driving Park & Fair Association.
W. M. K. & F. Ry. Depot.
X. H. & T. C. Ry. Depot.
Y. St. L. & Sw. Ry. Depot.
Z. S. A. & A. P. Ry. Depot.
    Odd Fellows Hall.
    Masonic Temple.
    Artesian Wells, daily flow 11,000,000 gal.

h. Public School Buildings.
c. Colored School Building.
r. Oil Works.
d. West End Fire Station.
e. East Waco Fire Station.
f. Central Fire Station.
g. The Blake Manufacturing Company.
h. Waco Cotton Mills.
i. Slayden Kinsey Woolen Mills.
j. Lone Star Cotton Manufactory.
k. Brazos Compress Co.
l. National Compress Co.
l. Waco Compress Co.
m. Brics Manufactory.
n. Foundry.

o. Carnitzeon's Foundry.
p. Stevenson's Manufacturing Co.
q. Waco Ice Refrigerating Co.
r. Waco Oil Works.
s. City Reservoir.
t. Waco Lumber Co.
u. Cameron Lumber Co.
v. Fougad & Blum Planing Mills.
w. Caroll's Creamery and Cannery.
x. Steam Laundry.
y. Bottling Works.
z. St. Louis & South Western Ft. Depot.
    Electric Street Ry.
    Population, 1892, 25,000.

WACO, TEXAS.

D. W. ENSIGN & CO.

1892.

SKETCHED BY A...

Waco, Texas, A. L. Westyard (1892). This map published by D. W. Ensign & Co. depicts Waco and the Brazos River. With the arrival of the railroad in 1871 and two more lines in the early 1880s, Waco became the central point of contact for local and regional cotton growers and small industries, connecting them to locales across Texas and the nation. In 1890 the city offered streetcars pulled by mules; electric cars partially replaced the mules in 1891. Waco is the seat of McLennan County.

MAP OF
TEXAS
AND PARTS OF
ADJOINING TERRITORIES

Compiled by and under the direction of
ROBERT T. HILL
Drawn by
Henry S. Selden and Willard D. Johnson

Natural provinces: [Texas], D. W. Ensign & Co. (1899?).
This map shows Texas, including the Indian Territory (Oklahoma) to the north and part of the Trans-Pecos area to the west. By 1899 Texas was almost completely marked by geographical boundaries. Most counties were, by this time, created and organized.

Map showing railroads and connecting lines of the Northern Texas Traction Co. from Ft. Worth to Dallas, Texas, compiled by Robert T. Hill (c 1905).

This circa 1905 map, compiled by Robert T. Hill, depicts the Northern Texas Traction Company line running between Dallas and Fort Worth. The NTT was one of several interurban electric railways in Texas. The NTT began operation on July 1, 1902. In 1905 Stone & Webster of Boston established the Northern Texas Electric Company and bought stock in NTT. The last run of the NTT was December 24, 1924.

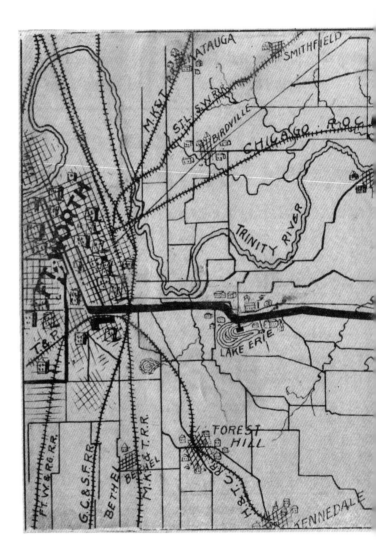

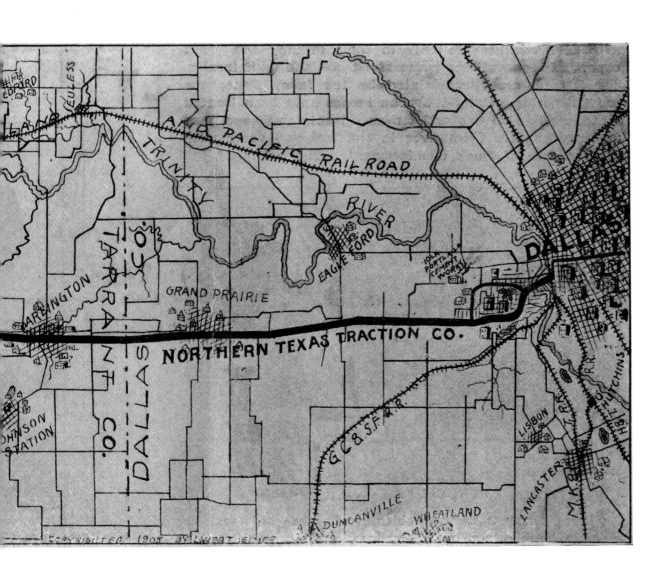

County map of Texas, and Indian Territory, published by Warner & Beers (1875).
This 1875 map of Texas shows Indian Territory to the north and Texas counties. West of 100° longitude is Bexar County, established in 1860, where San Antonio is the county seat. The state legislature eventually carved 128 counties from Bexar.

The Twentieth Century

THE POPULATION OF TEXAS ROSE 109 PERCENT during the thirty years from 1890 to 1920, growing from 2,235,527 people to 4,663,226. Most Texans continued living the rural lifestyle of the nineteenth century, but Texas was on the precipice of state-shaking change. That change came in the form of liquid gold. On January 1, 1901, oil was discovered on a salt dome formation south of Beaumont at a site called Spindletop. The well spewed an estimated one hundred thousand barrels a day until it was capped on January 19. More wells were dug on or near the site.

However, on the eve of the incipient oil boom, devastation hit Galveston. On the morning of September 8, 1900, a devastating storm tore through the young city. Some six thousand residents were killed, and more than half the buildings were in ruins.

In 1928 Texas became the leading oil-producing state in the nation, with some 256 million barrels. But on October 29, 1929, "Black Tuesday," the stock market crashed, bringing on the Great Depression. The large state newspapers shrugged and predicted that business would continue. However, the patina on the state's economy began to show wear as businesses failed and unemployment increased. Overproduction of oil in East Texas caused Governor Ross Sterling to declare martial law and shut down the fields. Oil dropped as low as two cents a barrel in 1931, and cotton prices stumbled to all-time lows, threatening production.

When Franklin Roosevelt assumed the presidency in 1933, he instituted "New Deal" programs designed to get the nation back on its feet. The Texas influence was felt on a national level because a number of Texans were serving in Washington. John Nance Garner was vice president; others chaired committees in the House and Senate. Through farm aid, for the first time farmers were paid to keep some crops out of production. More aid was required in the 1930s when dust storms ravaged the panhandle in what became known as the Dust Bowl.

With its vast open lands and suitable weather for training exercises, the Lone Star State became a mecca for military bases during World Wars I and II. Millions of dollars poured in to construct facilities at Fort Worth, Houston, San Antonio, and Waco. World War II brought a greater influx of military personnel into the state, requiring additional facilities. Defense and manufacturing plants spread throughout various parts of the state and contributed to its economy.

The Japanese attack on Pearl Harbor on December 7, 1941, rallied the American people to an unexpected patriotic fervor. Texas, with 5 percent of the nation's population, provided 7 percent of the military forces, some 750,000 troops. Of this number 22,022 died or suffered fatal battle wounds during World War II. The federal government poured millions of dollars into base construction, military hardware, and supplies. This amounted to half a billion dollars in 1941 alone and was a great shot in the economic arm of the state.

The petrochemical industry, located from Port Arthur to Corpus Christi, became the largest in the world following the war. Other industries such as steel mills, tin smelters, and paper and pulp processors became big business in East Texas. Although it started small, a harbinger of things to come in the economy of the Lone Star State was the advent of electronics. Texas Instruments was the first company to take advantage of the transistor. The postwar demand for workers brought about a mass exodus of people from rural communities to the cities, and by 1950 a majority of Texans, some 60 percent, resided in urban areas.

Harry Truman's ascendancy to the presidency following the death of Roosevelt changed politics and cultural aspects of the nation forever, as well as raising dissension in Texas and other Southern states. He integrated the military services, forbade discrimination in federal hiring, and advocated elimination of the poll tax. During the presidential campaign of 1952, staunchly Democratic Texas chose to back the Republican nominee, the popular World War II leader Dwight Eisenhower. The main appeal of "Ike" in Texas was his promise to "'return' the tidelands to Texas and respect states' rights in general."

The Democratic nominee, Adlai Stevenson, made no such promises and was viewed as part of the "mess in Washington." One of the first acts signed by Eisenhower upon becoming president was a bill guaranteeing state ownership of the tidelands, which meant a monetary windfall for both the state and the oil companies.

Racial discrimination still reared its ugly head in postwar Texas. Blacks and those of Mexican descent suffered from poor schools, unequal representation in politics, lack of voting rights, and other discrimination. Changes were on the horizon, however. In 1956 Henry B. Gonzalez became the first Mexican-American elected to the Texas Senate. He made an unsuccessful bid for governor in 1958 but later became the first of his ancestry elected to the U.S. House of Representatives. Slowly, other minorities began to move upward in state affairs. Barbara Jordan won a seat in the Texas Senate in 1966 and in 1972 became the first black woman from the South elected to the U.S. House of Representatives.

The Vietnam War was as loudly protested in Texas as elsewhere. When President John F. Kennedy was assassinated in Dallas in November 1963, his successor, Lyndon Baines Johnson, a Texan, escalated the war and drew even more hatred and demonstrations even in his own state. The bitterness was so deep from many sectors of the American public that Johnson declined to run for reelection.

Politics dominated the final thirty years of the twentieth century in Texas. William Clements won the governorship in 1978, becoming the first Republican to reach that pinnacle in more than a century; his election also marked the emergence of Texas as a two-party state for the first time since Reconstruction. Democrats won the governor's chair in 1982 and 1990, while Republicans took the prize in 1986, 1994, and 1998. John Tower became the first Republican elected senator from Texas since Reconstruction, and George W. Bush defeated Ann Richards for governor, setting the stage for his presidential candidacy.

In the 1970s and 1980s, Texas became emblazoned on the American id. While the rest of the country was either stagnant in growth or going backwards, Texas prosperity not only brought an increase in population, it also brought on a near-cult following. "All things Texas" became the fad of the day, from boots to shirts; country and western music crossed elitist barriers; movies and television put more Texas into the public mind. Sports made its contribution to the Texas aura, especially in the form of the Dallas Cowboys, "America's Team."

While oil production remained at a low point in the 1990s, other industries moved in. High-tech firms saw Texas as an ideal location for research and development; employment in electronics increased 55 percent. The North American Free Trade Agreement (NAFTA) that the United States, Mexico, and Canada signed in 1992 became a bonus in billions of dollars in trade with Mexico.

At decade's end Texas's population stood at 20,851,820, supplanting New York as number two in standing and trailing only California.

Now, nearly ten years into the twenty-first century, the number of people has continued to grow at a rate double the national average. The state's residents are becoming older, less rural, and more diverse, but they remain as much a part of the Texas identity as those who came before.

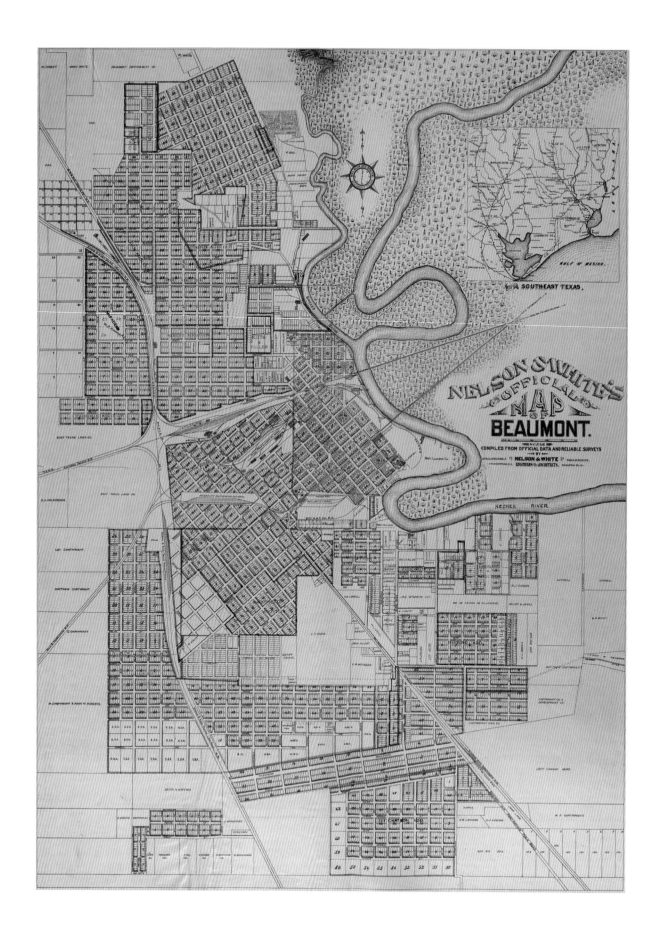

Beaumont, Texas, Nelson & White (1902).
Oil was discovered at nearby Spindletop in 1901 and changed the historic Gulf Coast town of Beaumont, founded in the 1830s, forever. Between January and March 1901, Beaumont's population grew from nine thousand to thirty thousand. Oil continues to be a major export of the industrial city on the gulf.

This monument is placed on the bridge to mark the limit of jurisdiction of the two Countries thereon in accordance with Article IV of the Treaty of 1884. Its location does not affect the boundary in the river, which remains in, and moves with, the center of the normal channel whether it is under the monument or not.

The monument stands on the down stream truss of the draw span just to the west of the post over the center of the draw pier.

Boundaries between Brownsville, Texas and Matamoros, Tam. (Mexico), Norris Peters Co. (1910).

This map presents an exaggerated flow of the Rio Grande River. Its true flow is much straighter, going from the northwest to the southeast, emptying into the Gulf of Mexico. While they are difficult to distinguish on the map, Brownsville is at the extreme end of the river on the north side, and Matamoros is across the river on the south side, where the Rio Grande flows into the Gulf.

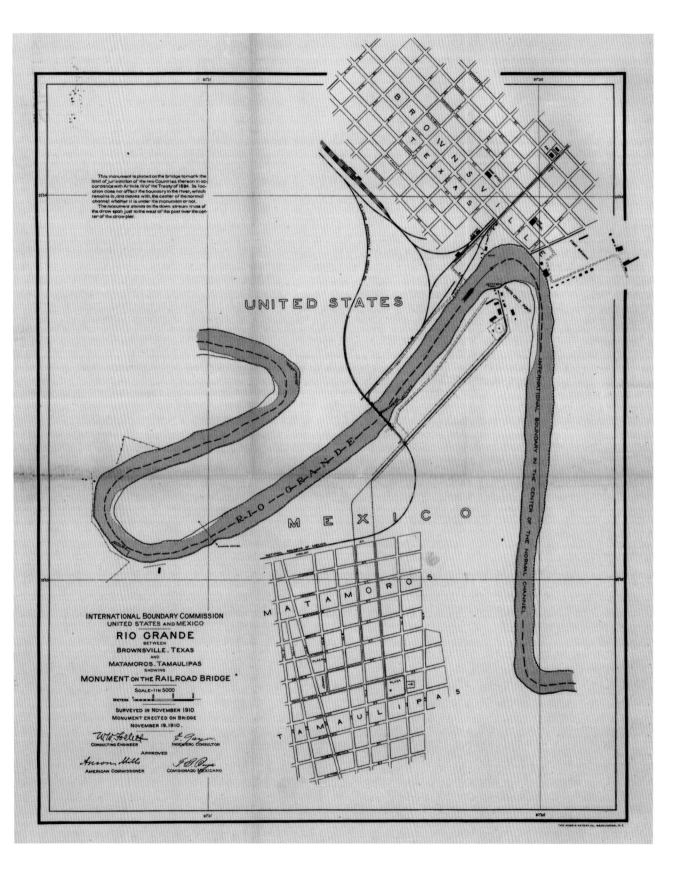

This monument is placed on the bridge to mark the limit of jurisdiction of the two Countries thereon in accordance with Article IV of the Treaty of 1884. Its location does not affect the boundary in the river, which remains in, and moves with, the center of the normal channel whether it is under the monument or not.

The monument stands on the down stream truss of the draw span just to the west of the post over the center of the draw pier.

UNITED STATES

RIO GRANDE

MEXICO

BROWNSVILLE

MATAMOROS

TAMAULIPAS

INTERNATIONAL BOUNDARY IN THE CENTER OF THE NORMAL CHANNEL

INTERNATIONAL BOUNDARY COMMISSION
UNITED STATES AND MEXICO
RIO GRANDE
BETWEEN
BROWNSVILLE, TEXAS
AND
MATAMOROS, TAMAULIPAS
SHOWING
MONUMENT ON THE RAILROAD BRIDGE

SCALE·1 IN 5000

METERS

SURVEYED IN NOVEMBER 1910
MONUMENT ERECTED ON BRIDGE
NOVEMBER 19, 1910.

CONSULTING ENGINEER   INGENIERO CONSULTOR

APPROVED

AMERICAN COMMISSIONER   COMISIONADO MEXICANO

THE NORRIS PETERS CO., WASHINGTON, D.C.

Within the image:
HOUSTON SHIP CHANNEL

AUDITORIUM

RICE HOTEL

ST JEAN HOTEL

STOWERS FURNITURE COMPANY

BENDER HOTEL

NEW BEATTY BLDG

BURNETT HOTEL

MAIN ST.

PRAIRIE ST.

WALKER AVE

FANNIN ST

RUSK AV

DRAWN BY
Hopkins & Motter
814 STEWART BLDG.
HOUSTON TEX.
COPYRIGHT 1912
ALL RIGHTS RESERVED

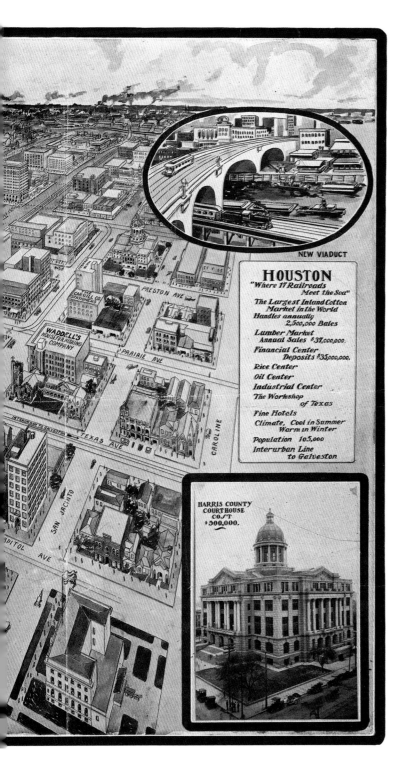

NEW VIADUCT

HOUSTON
"Where 17 Railroads
Meet the Sea"
The Largest Inland Cotton
Market in the World
Handles annually
2,500,000 Bales
Lumber Market
Annual Sales $37,000,000.
Financial Center
Deposits $35,000,000.
Rice Center
Oil Center
Industrial Center
The Workshop
of Texas
Fine Hotels
Climate, Cool in Summer
Warm in Winter
Population 105,000
Interurban Line
to Galveston

HARRIS COUNTY
COURTHOUSE
COST
$500,000.

Houston—a modern city, Hopkins & Motter (1912).

This 1912 map of Houston gives an indication of the growth possibilities of the city. The site was founded and named for the hero of San Jacinto in hopes of making a profit off land sales. Sam Houston preferred his namesake city as the capital of the republic and disliked Austin, going so far as to having the republic's records "confiscated" from their offices in Austin.

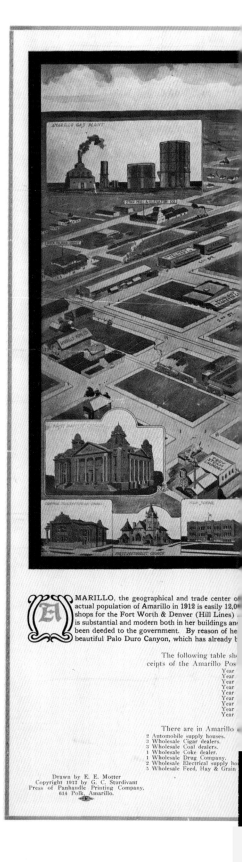

Aeroplane view of business district Amarillo, Texas, drawn by E. E. Motter (1912).

This 1912 map of Amarillo shows a growing and prosperous city. The town, located in the Great Plains section of the Texas Panhandle, overflows into two counties. It became a center for oil and ranching, as well as other industries in the region. Today the population is around two hundred fifty thousand.

AEROPLANE VIEW OF BUSINESS DISTRICT AMARILLO, TEXAS

...uare miles of the Texas Panhandle and a still larger area of Eastern New Mexico, and Western Oklahoma, had **9,957** population inside the corporate limits by the 1910 census. The ...e has never been a cessation in her growth. Amarillo has three transcontinental railway systems, with vast shops, offices and terminal facilities of the Santa Fe and with division offices and ...land. Amarillo has a Federal court, weather bureau, Court of Civil Appeals. Amarillo's school, church and college property aggregates over a million dollars in value. Amarillo's growth ...strial, commercial, social and civic enterprises. Congress has authorized an appropriation of $250,000 for the erection of a Federal building on a site valued at $10,000 which has already ...altitude, 3700 feet above sea level, Amarillo enjoys a life-giving atmosphere which attracts many visitors and many residents from less favored climes. Fifteen miles south of the city lies the ...ture's playground of national fame.

...stant and remarkable growth of the total re-
...a period of 9 years:

...........................$10,911.94
...........................12,545.57
...........................12,859.92
...........................17,502.08
...........................25,376.70
...........................33,525.04
...........................42,627.78
...........................49,786.64
...........................47,932.96

...g wholesale and jobbing houses:—

1 Wholesale Fruit and Produce company.
4 Wholesale Grocers.
2 Wholesale Hardware houses.
1 Wholesale Paints, Oil, & Painters' supplies house.
3 Wholesale Gasoline and oil establishments.
2 Wholesale plumbing concerns.
2 Wholesale well machinery and supply houses.

The following is a list of Amarillo's manufacturing enterprises.

3 Artificial Stone manufacturers.	1 Fireproof metal window factory.
2 Bottling Works.	1 Furniture and mattress factory.
1 Brick and tile factory.	1 Gas plant.
1 Broom factory.	3 Grain elevators.
1 Cabinet shop.	1 Harness and Saddlery manufacturer.
2 Candy factories.	3 Ice Cream factories.
1 Carriage and wagon factory.	2 Ice factories.
1 Cigar factory.	3 Steam Laundries.
1 Candy wagon factory.	2 Marble works.
2 Flour and meal mills.	3 Planing mills.
3 Cornice manufacturers.	1 Sash and door factory.
2 Creameries.	3 Tank factories.
2 Electric sign factories.	1 Vulcanizing plant.
4 Chop and feed mills.	1 Water, Light & Power Plant.

Here are the accurate government figures showing the percentage of population gain of the fastest growing cities in the United States during the past decade:—

AMARILLO, TEXAS .... 590 per cent

Oklahoma City, Okla .... 540 per cent		Monessen, Penna .... 437 per cent
N. Yakima, Wash. .... 346 per cent		Aberdeen, Wash .... 265 per cent
Virginia, Minn. .... 254 per cent		Birmingham, Ala .... 245 per cent
Salem, Ore .... 231 per cent		Everett, Wash. .... 215 per cent
Los Angeles, Cal .... 211 per cent		Billings, Mont. .... 210 per cent

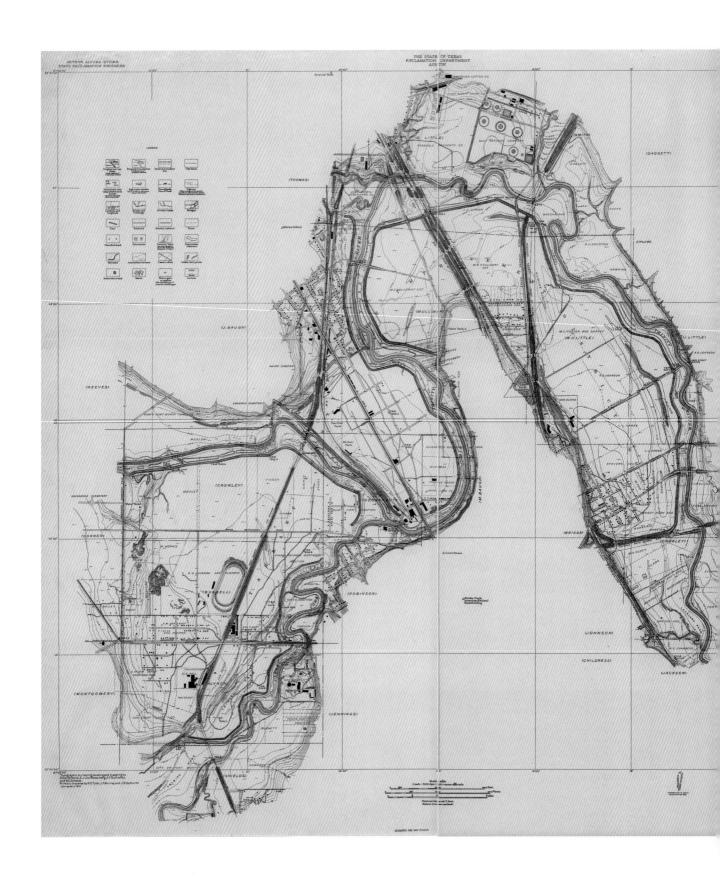

Texas: MAPPING THE LONE STAR STATE THROUGH HISTORY

Tarrant County, Trinity River, Fort Worth sheet. The state of Texas, Reclamation Department;
topographic surveying, leveling, and mapping by Dixon B. Penick . . . [et al.]; primary traverse
by R. G. Tyler, J. P. Murray, and J. B. Upchurch (1915).
Fort Worth ("Cowtown") is almost the center of Tarrant County, and the Trinity River flows through town.
Originally established as a site for a military fort, today the city is a bustling place with a population of more
than six hundred thousand.

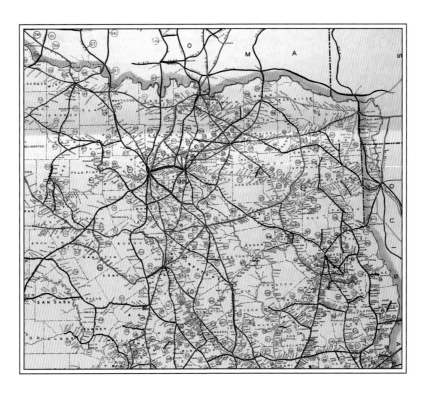

Railroad map of Texas, compiled and issued by Ira D. Dodge (1926).
By the mid-1920s, there was a vast network of railways crossing the state. Although
railroad construction in the state had stopped with the outbreak of the Civil War,
it resumed after the war, and by 1888 there were some 8,000 miles of operating
track, with more laid each day. Today over 10,000 miles of track cross the state,
and Texas ranks second to Illinois in carloads and fifth in freight tons carried.

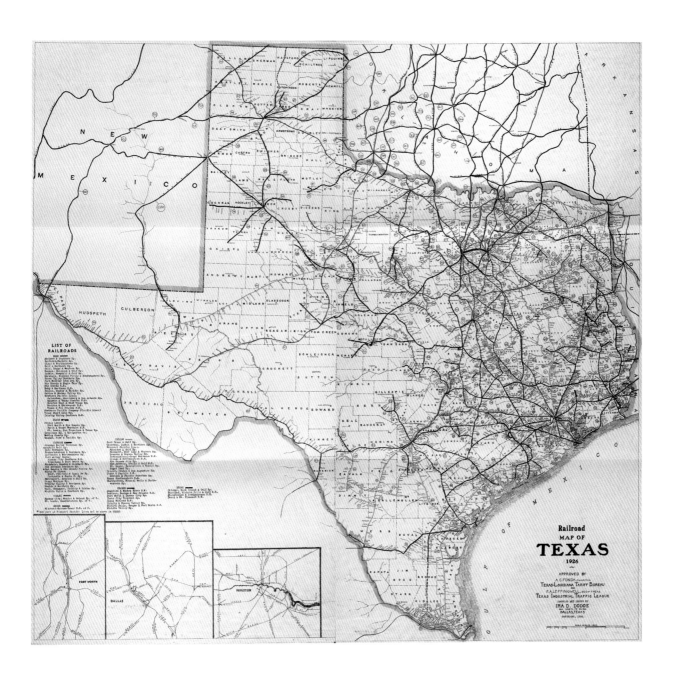

LIST OF RAILROADS

Railroad
MAP OF
TEXAS
1926

APPROVED BY

A.C. FONDA, CHAIRMAN
TEXAS-LOUISIANA TARIFF BUREAU

F.A. LEFFINGWELL, SECRETARY
TEXAS INDUSTRIAL TRAFFIC LEAGUE

COMPILED AND ISSUED BY
IRA D. DODGE
200 SANTA FE BLDG.
DALLAS, TEXAS
COPYRIGHT, 1926

Pictorial map of San Antonio, Fanita Lanier (1935).
This pictorial map depicts the city of San Antonio in 1935. The Alamo City, rich in history, was once the capital of Spanish Texas and is located in the south-central section of the state. The city's nickname comes from San Antonio de Valero, the oldest Spanish mission in San Antonio, built in 1718 and more popularly known as the Alamo.

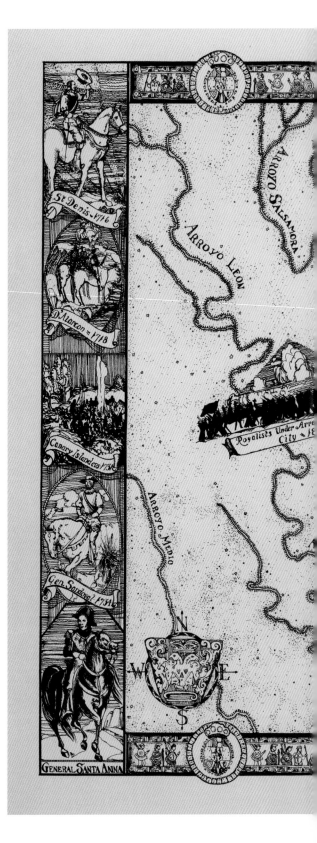

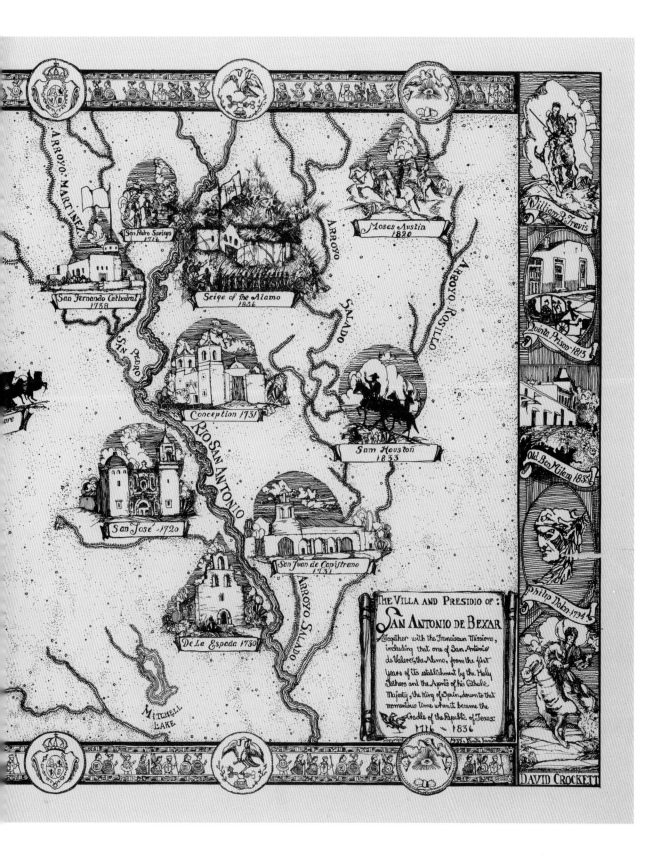

THE VILLA AND PRESIDIO OF:
SAN ANTONIO DE BEXAR
Together with the Franciscan Missions, including that one of San Antonio de Valero, the Alamo, from the first years of its establishment by the Holy Fathers and the Agents of his Catholic Majesty, the King of Spain, down to that momentous Time when it became the Cradle of the Republic of Texas: 1716 – 1836

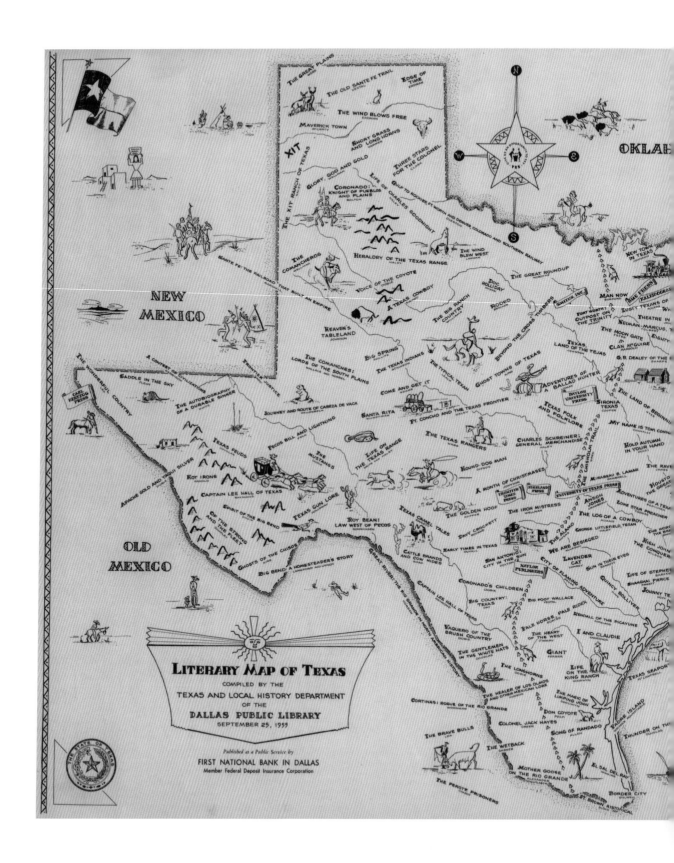

LITERARY MAP OF TEXAS

COMPILED BY THE

TEXAS AND LOCAL HISTORY DEPARTMENT

OF THE

DALLAS PUBLIC LIBRARY

SEPTEMBER 25, 1955

Published as a Public Service by

FIRST NATIONAL BANK IN DALLAS

Member Federal Deposit Insurance Corporation

Literary map of Texas, compiled Sept. 25, 1955, First National Bank in Texas (1955).

From Edna Ferber's classic *Giant* to the biography of Charles Goodnight to the story of "Shanghai Pierce," one of the more colorful figures in Texas ranch history, this map celebrates the diversity of the Texas literary tradition and the spirit of Texas itself.

Color image map: [ports of entry, United States-Mexican border], produced by the U.S. Geological Survey in cooperation with the Department of the Treasury, U.S. Customs Service (1979).

The border between the United States and Mexico has generally been open, restricted only by customs checks at points of entry. However, as of June 1, 2009, a passport or some similar high-tech document is now required to cross from either side of the border through those checkpoints.

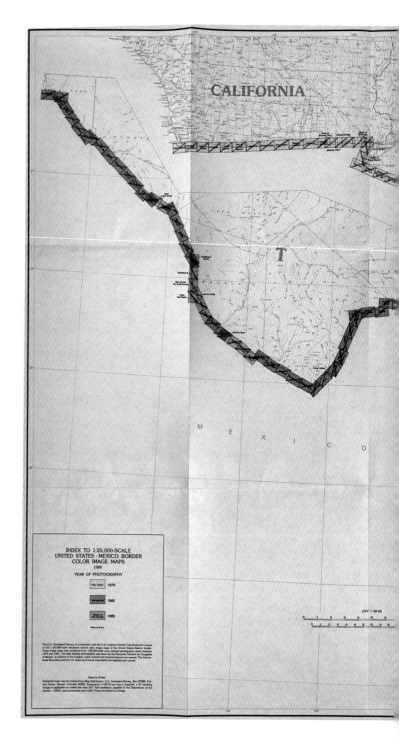

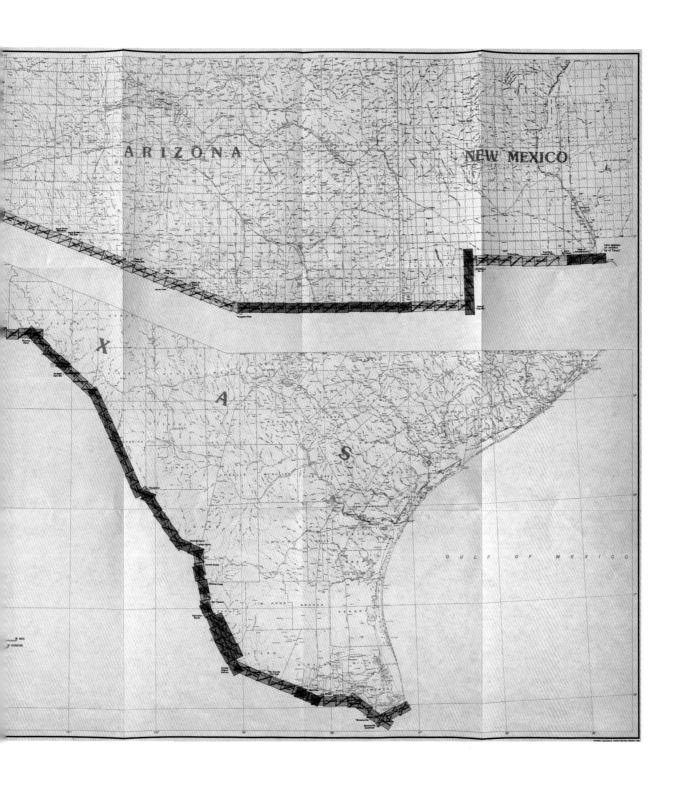

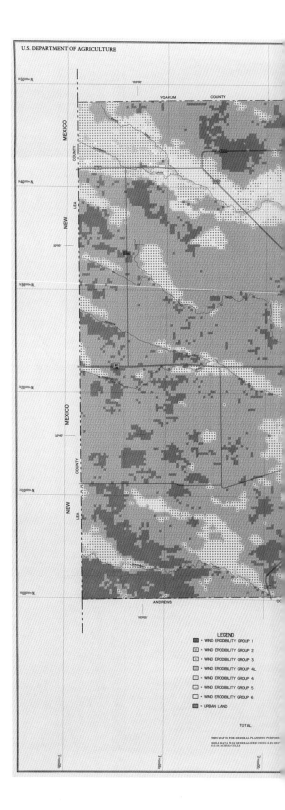

Interpretative map of wind erodibility. Gaines County, Texas.
U.S. Department of Agriculture, Soil Conservation Service,
Temple, Texas, cooperating with Texas Natural Resources
Information System, Austin, Texas (1986).

Gaines County, situated on the south end of the High Plains of West Texas, suffered greatly through the Dust Bowl of the 1930s as high winds swept away valuable topsoil. This map pertains to the enterprise of farming in the dry, highly erodible soil of the area. In addition to producing wheat, cotton, and sorghum, Gaines County is also an oil-rich area.

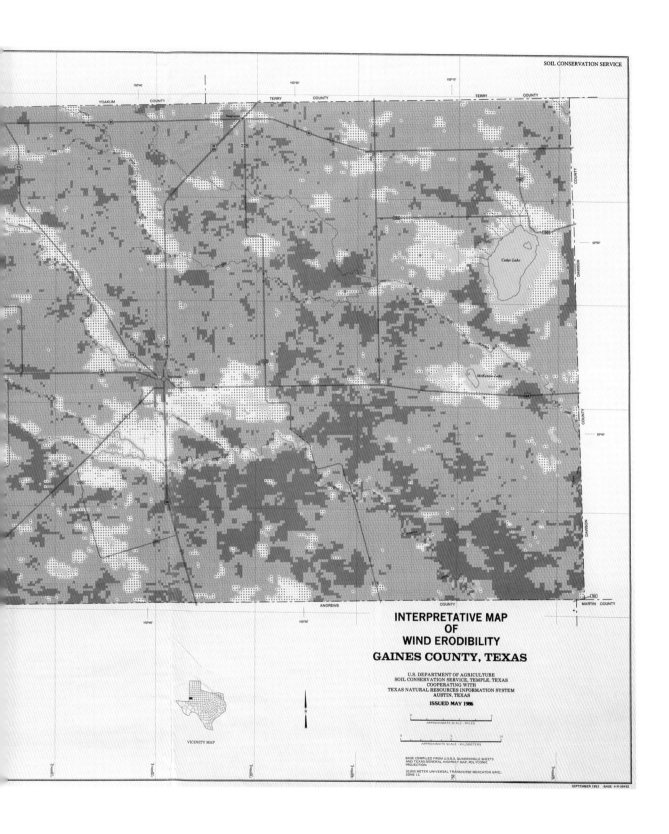

SOIL CONSERVATION SERVICE

**INTERPRETATIVE MAP
OF
WIND ERODIBILITY**

GAINES COUNTY, TEXAS

U.S. DEPARTMENT OF AGRICULTURE
SOIL CONSERVATION SERVICE, TEMPLE, TEXAS
COOPERATING WITH
TEXAS NATURAL RESOURCES INFORMATION SYSTEM
AUSTIN, TEXAS
ISSUED MAY 1986

APPROXIMATE SCALE - MILES

APPROXIMATE SCALE - KILOMETERS

BASE COMPILED FROM U.S.G.S. QUADRANGLE SHEETS
AND TEXAS GENERAL HIGHWAY MAP, POLYCONIC
PROJECTION.

10,000 METER UNIVERSAL TRANSVERSE MERCATOR GRID,
ZONE 13.

SEPTEMBER 1983   BASE 4-R-38442

VICINITY MAP

All maps come from the Library of Congress Geography and Map Division unless otherwise noted. To order reproductions of Library of Congress items, please contact the Library of Congress Photoduplication Service, Washington, D.C. 20540-4570 or call 202-707-5640.

Page viii Ruysch, Johann. "Universalior cogniti orbis tabula." In Claudius Ptolmeus, *Geographia*. Rome, 1507. G1005 1507.W3 Vault.

Page ix Waldseemüller, Martin. "Universalis cosmographia secundum Ptholmaei traditionem et Americi Vespucci alioru[m] que lustrations," St. Dié, France? 1507. G3200 1507.W3 Vault.

Page 4 Schenk, Peter. Tabula Mexicae et Floridae: terrarum Anglicarum, et anteriorum Americae insularum, item cursuum et circuituum fluminis Mississipi dicti. G3300 1710 .S3.

Page 8 Senex, John. A map of Louisiana and of the river Mississipi [i.e., Mississippi]: this map of the Mississipi [i.e., Mississippi] is most humbly inscribed to William Law of Lanreston, esq. by Iohn Senex. [London: Printed for Daniel Browne . . . , 1721] G3700 1721 .S4 Vault.

Pages 10–11 Carte de la côte de la Louisiane depuis la Baye St. Joseph, jusqu'à celle de St. Bernard où tous les ports et bons mouillages sont marquez par des ancres; avec la quantité de piés d'eau que l'on y trouve. [1732?] G3862.C6 1732 .C3 Vault.

Page 9 Bowen, Emanuel. A new & accurate map of Louisiana, with part of Florida and Canada, and the adjacent countries. Drawn from surveys, assisted by the most approved English & French maps & charts, the whole being regulated by astronl. observations. [London, 1752] G3300 1752 .B6 Vault.

Pages 12–13 Sánchez, Josef María. Plano del Lago de San Bernardo en el Seno Mexicano, delineado pr. Dn. Josef María Sánchez, pilotin del numero del Departamto. de Cádiz, vaxo la corrección de Dn. Pedro Revelles, maestro delineador pr. S.M. [1783] G4032.S26 1783 .S2 Vault.

Pages 14–15 Luffman, J. A map of North America; Outline of North America, in correspond to the map. [1803] G3300 1803 .L8 TIL.

Page 16 Bruff, Joseph Goldsborough. Provincias internas del reyno de Nuevo España [1846] G4430 179- .B7 Vault.

Pages 22–23 Austin, Stephen F. Mapa topográfico de la provincia de Texas. [1822?] G4030 1822 .A9 Vault TIL.

Pages 24–25 Young, J. H. (James Hamilton). New map of Texas: with the contiguous American & Mexican states. Philadelphia: S. Augustus Mitchell, 1835. G4030 1835 .Y6.

Page 26 Tanner, Henry Schenck. Map of Texas with parts of the adjoining states, compiled by Stephen F. Austin. Philadelphia: H. S. Tanner, 1837 (Philadelphia: John & Wm. W. Warr, engravers). G4030 1837 .T3 Vault.

Page 27 Gilman, E. Sketch of Texas with the boundaries of Mexican States as shown on General Austin's map of Texas published by R. S. Tanner, 1839. G4030 1839 .G5 TIL Vault.

Page 28 Standidge & Co. Map of Texas. [S.l., 184–?] G4030 184– .S7 TIL.

Page 29 Arrowsmith, John. Map of Texas, compiled from surveys recorded in the Land Office of Texas and other official surveys. London: John Arrowsmith, 1841. G4030 1841 .A7 Vault.

Pages 30–31 Gray, A. B. (Andrew Belcher). Map of the river Sabine from Logan's Ferry to 32nd degree of north latitude: shewing the boundary between the United States of America and the Republic of Texas between said points, as marked and laid down by survey in 1841, under the direction of the Joint Commission appointed for that purpose under the 1st article of the convention signed at Washington on the 25th day of April 1838, drawn by A. B. Gray. [United States?: s.n., 1842?] G4032.S15 1842 .G7.

Pages 32–33 United States Topographical Bureau. Map of Texas and the countries adjacent, 1844. G4030 1844 .U5 TIL.

Page 34 Mitchell, S. Augustus (Samuel Augustus). A new map of Texas, Oregon and California. [S.l.], 1846. G4050 1846 .M5 TIL.

Page 39 Texas, nach den besten Quellen entw. u. gez. vom Hauptm. Radefeld. Hildburghausen: Stich, Druck und Verlag des Bibliographischen Instituts. [1846] G4030 1846 .T4 Vault.

Pages 40–41 Berlandier, Luis. Plan of the ground situated to the north of Matamoras between the Rio Bravo & the Arroyo Colorado, by Luis Berlandier, membro de la commission de geografia militar. [1846] G4032.L75S44 1846 .B4 Vault.

Pages 42–43 Disturnell, John. Mapa de los Estados Unidos de Méjico: segun lo organizado y definido por las varias actas del congreso de dicha république y construido por las mejores autoridades. New York: J. Disturnell, 1847. G4410 1847 .D5 Vault.

Pages 44–45 Emory, William H. (William Hemsley). Boundary between the United States and Mexico. [Washington, D.C., 1855] G3701.F2 1855 .E6 TIL.

Page 46–47 Pope, John. From the Red River to the Rio Grande from explorations and surveys made under the direction of the Hon. Jefferson Davis, Secretary of War, by Captain John Pope, Corps Topl. Engrs. assisted by Lieutenant Kenner Gerrard, 1st Dragoons, 1854–6. [Washington, D.C., 1859] G4031.P25 1856 .P6 RR 171.

Pages 48–49 Warren, Gouverneur Kemble. Map of the military dep't of Texas: being a section of the map of the territory of the U.S. from the Mississippi River to the Pacific Ocean, compiled from all the reliable data by Lt. G. K. Warren, T.E., under the direction of Capt. A. A. Humphreys, T.E.; lith. of J. Bien. [Washington, D.C.?]: Office Expl.ns and Surveys, War Dep't, 1859. G4030 1859 .W3.

Page 50 Bachmann, John. Panorama of the seat of war: bird's eye view of Texas and part of Mexico, drawn from nature and lith. by John Bachmann. New York: John Bachmann, Publisher. [1861] G4031.A35 1861 .B2 Vault: CW 446.8.

Pages 54–55 Gentry, A. M. Map of Texas, showing the line of the Texas and New Orleans Rail Road, and its connections in the U.S. and adjacent territories. [n.p.], 1860. G3936.P3 1860 .G4 RR 577.

Pages 56–57 Colton, J. H. (Joseph Hutchins). Colton's United States shewing the military stations, forts, &c. Prepared by J. H. Colton, New York, for the "Rebellion Record." New York: G. P. Putnam, 1861. G3700 1861 .C685 CW 7.5.

Pages 58–59 Cushing, E. H. Campaign map of Texas, Louisiana and Arkansas, showing all the battle fields and also the marches of Walker's Division [1861–65]. Entered according to Act of Congress in the year 1871 by E. H. Cushing. Engraved, printed and manufactured by G. W. & C. B. Colton & Co., New York. Houston, Texas. J. P. Blessington, 16 Tex. Vol. Inf. 1871. G3991. S5 1871 .C8 CW 63.

Page 60 Texas Coast showing points of occupation of expedition under Maj. Gen. N. P. Banks: Nov'r 1863. [1863?] G4032.C6S5 1863 .T4 Vault: CW 447.

Pages 64–65 Haupt, Lewis M. (Lewis Muhlenberg). Map of the post of Fort Brown, Brownsville, Texas, surveyed and drawn under the direction of B'vt Maj. Genl. E. R. S. Canby, commanding fifth military district by L. M. Haupt, 2nd Lieut. U.S. Corp. of Engineers, March 1869. [1877] G4034.B8:2F6 1877 .H3 Vault.

Pages 66–67 Schönberg & Co. Schönberg's map of Texas. [New York: Schönberg & Co., 1866] G4030 1866 .S3 Vault.

Pages 68–69 Colton, G. Woolworth. Colton's new map of the state of Texas: the Indian Territory and adjoining portions of New Mexico, Louisiana, and Arkansas, compiled from the official county maps of the General Land Office, the personal reconnaisances and geological explorations of Prof. A. R. Roessler, the surveys of the Mexican Boundary Commission, U.S. Coast Surveys, U.S. General Land Office, the various Rail Road Cos., information furnished by Mr. Pressler, and other authentic materials by G. Woolworth Colton. New York: G. W. & C. B. Colton & Co., 1872. G4030 1872 .C6 Vault.

Pages 70–71 G. W. & C. B. Colton & Co. Map of the state of Texas showing the line and lands of the Texas and Pacific Railway reserved and donated by the State of Texas. New York, 1873. G4031.P3 1873 .G15 RR 578.

Pages 72–73 Bien, Julius, 1826–1909. Corpus Christi and Rio Grande Railway Company [map showing the proposed railroad between Laredo and Corpus Christi and its connections with Mexico]. New York. [1874] G4031.P3 1873 .B5 RR 393.

Pages 74–75 G. W. & C. B. Colton & Co. Texas and Pacific Railway and its connections. New York, 1876. G3701.P3 1876 .G15 RR 579.

Pages 76–77 G. W. & C. B. Colton & Co. Neue Karte de Staates Texas für 1881. G4030 1881 .G3 TIL.

Pages 78–79 Island City Abstract and Loan Co. Map of the county and city of Galveston, Texas, compiled from original field notes and latest surveys. Galveston, Tex.: Island City Abstract and Loan Co., 1891. G4033.G25 1891 .I4.

Pages 80–81 Giraud, Paul, del. & sculp. Dallas, Texas. With the projected river and navigation improvements viewed from above the sister city of Oak Cliff. Dallas Lith. Co., 1892. G4034. D2A3 1892 .G5.

Pages 82–83 Westyard, A. L. Waco, Texas, 1892. [n.p.] D. W. Ensign & Co. [1892]. G4034. W2A3 1892 .W4.

Pages 84–85 Map of Texas and parts of adjoining territories, compiled by and under the direction of Robert T. Hill; drawn by Henry S. Selden and Willard D. Johnson, 1899; Andrew B. Graham Co., photo-lithographers, Washington, D.C. [1899?] G4031.C21 1899.N2 Vault.

Pages 86–87 Northern Texas Traction Co. [Map showing railroads and connecting lines of the Northern Texas Traction Co. from Ft. Worth to Dallas, Texas]. [Cleveland, Ohio]: L. Wertheimer, c1905. G4034.F7P3 1905 .N6 Vault.

Page 88 H. H. Lloyd & Co. County map of Texas, and Indian Territory. Chicago, Ill.: Warner. [1875] G4030 1875 .H2.

Pages 92–93 Nelson & White's official map of Beaumont: compiled from official data and reliable surveys, by Nelson & White; O. M. Simpson, B.S.C.E.; W. R. Kaufman, del. Beaumont, TX: Nelson & White, [1902?]. G4031.B3 1902.N4.

Pages 94–95 International Boundary Commission, United States & Mexico. Boundaries between Brownsville, Texas and Matamoros, Tam. (Mexico) [Washington, D.C.: The Norris Peters Co., 1910]. G3701.F2 1910 .I6 TIL.

Pages 96–97 Hopkins & Motter. Houston—a modern city. Houston, c1912. G4034.H8A3 1912 .H6.

Pages 98–99 Motter, E. E. Aeroplane view of business district Amarillo, Texas. Drawn by E. E. Motter. Copyright by G. C. Sturdivant. Amarillo, Panhandle Printing Company, c1912. G4034.A5A3 1912 .M6.

Pages 100–101 Texas. Reclamation Dept. Tarrant County, Trinity River, Fort Worth sheet. The state of Texas, Reclamation Department; topographic surveying, leveling, and mapping by Dixon B. Penick . . . [et al.]; primary traverse by R. G. Tyler, J. P. Murray, and J. B. Upchurch. (Austin: Engraved and printed by the U.S. Geological Survey, 1915.) G4032.T78J4 1915 .T4 Vault.

Pages 102–103 Dodge, Ira D. Railroad map of Texas, 1926, compiled and issued by Ira D. Dodge. (Dallas: Ira D. Dodge, 1926.) G4031. P3 1926 .D6.

Pages 104–105 Lanier, Fanita. The villa and presidio of San Antonio de Bexar: together with the Franciscan Missions, including that one of San Antonio de Valero, the Alamo, from the first years of its establishment by the holy fathers and the agents of his Catholic Majesty, the King of Spain, down to that momentous time when it became the cradle of the republic of Texas, 1716–1836. [1935] G4031.S5 1935.L3.

Pages 106–107 Dallas. Public Library. Texas and Local History Dept. Literary map of Texas. Compiled Sept. 25, 1955. [Dallas] First National Bank in Dallas. [1955] G4031.E65 1955 .D3.

Page 108–109 U.S. Geological Survey, Color image map: [ports of entry, United States-Mexican border], produced by the U.S. Geological Survey in cooperation with the Department of the Treasury, U.S. Customs Service. (Reston, VA: The Survey, 1979.) G3701.F2 s25 .G4.

Pages 110–111 United States Soil Conservation Service, Interpretative map of wind erodibility. Gaines County, Texas. U.S. Department of Agriculture, Soil Conservation Service, Temple, Texas, cooperating with Texas Natural Resources Information System, Austin, Texas. (USDA-SCS-National Cartographic Center: Fort Worth, 1986) G4033.G2J15 1986 .U5.

Acknowledgments

The publisher and the authors gratefully acknowledge the staff at the Library of Congress for their fine work and research assistance on this book, particularly Aimee Hess, Ralph Eubanks, and Colleen Cahill.

Without the vision and professionalism of Erin Turner at The Globe Pequot Press, this audacious project would not be the permanent achievement it is bound to be.

—VINCENT VIRGA
—DON BLEVINS

About the Authors

VINCENT VIRGA Critically acclaimed for *Cartographia: Mapping Civilization*, Vincent Virga also coauthored *Eyes of the Nation: A Visual History of the United States* with the Library of Congress and Alan Brinkley. Among his other books are *The Eighties: Images of America* with a foreword by Richard Rhodes; *Eisenhower: A Centennial Life* with text by Michael Beschloss; and *The American Civil War: 365 Days* with Gary Gallagher and Margaret Wagner. He has been hailed as "America's foremost picture editor" for having researched, edited, and designed nearly 150 picture sections in books by authors who include John Wayne, Jane Fonda, Arianna Huffington, Walter Cronkite, Hillary Clinton, and Bill Clinton. Virga edited *Forcing Nature: Trees in Los Angeles*, photographs by George Haas for Vincent Virga Editions. He is the author of six novels, including *Gaywyck*, *Vadriel Vail*, and *A Comfortable Corner*, as well as publisher of ViVa Editions. He has a Web site through the Authors Guild at www.vincentvirga.com.

DON BLEVINS has a master's degree in southwestern studies from Texas State University. He is a member of the Texas State Historical Association and the Writers' League of Texas. Don has written articles for more than fifty magazines, including *True West*, *American History Illustrated*, *German Life*, and *The Old Farmer's Almanac*. Don has authored four books: *Peculiar, Uncertain, and Two Egg*; *From Angels to Hellcats*; *Texas Towns: From Abner to Zipperlandville*; and *A Priest, A Prostitute, and Some Other Early Texans*. Don resides in San Marcos, Texas, with his wife.